COMING TO AGE

COMING TO AGE

GROWING OLDER
WITH POETRY

Edited by
MARY ANN HOBERMAN
and
CAROLYN HOPLEY

LITTLE, BROWN AND COMPANY

New York Boston London

Little, Brown and Company
Hachette Book Group
1290 Avenue of the Americas, New York, NY 10104
littlebrown.com

First Edition: April 2020

Little, Brown and Company is a division of Hachette Book Group, Inc.
The Little, Brown name and logo are trademarks of
Hachette Book Group, Inc.

The publisher is not responsible for websites (or their content) that are not
owned by the publisher.

The Hachette Speakers Bureau provides a wide range of authors for speaking
events. To find out more, go to hachettespeakersbureau.com or call
(866) 376-6591.

ISBN 978-0-316-42491-2
LCCN 2019951043

10 9 8 7 6 5 4 3 2 1

LSC-C

Printed in the United States of America

CONTENTS

To our readers:
May poetry enrich their lives,
as it has ours,
as they come to age.

COMING TO AGE

INTRODUCTION

This book started with a single, simple idea. We would gather together a group of poems that dealt with the subject of age and aging. Because we ourselves had found inspiration and joy in poetry throughout our lives, we thought that others would, too, particularly if it dealt with the existential questions that occupy us ever more urgently as we grow older.

The title came to us as a play on words. The familiar expression "coming of age" refers to that stage of life when one enters into adulthood, leaving youth for maturity. Coming *to* age suggests something other, an arrival rather than a departure. Entering this last stage, each newcomer may experience it differently. Yeats dwelled on his lost youth; Milosz celebrated his newfound fellowship.

If we are fortunate enough to live into our later years, we come to know what old age is firsthand. What does that mean? We have or will soon become founding members of the "old old," now the fastest growing segment of the over-sixty-five population. At eighty the novelist Penelope Lively wrote: "Our experience is one unknown to most of humanity, over time. We are the pioneers." And if we are pioneers, we owe it to those who follow to make something worthwhile of our good fortune.

Just as we read newspapers for news of the world, we read poetry for news of ourselves. Poets, particularly those who have lived and written into old age, have much to tell us. But along with acquiring new insights from their poems, we are reminded of what we already know. A line, a phrase, or even a single word, placed in the right context, can illuminate some part of our own experience, revealing a deeper significance, even a spiritual sustenance.

Reading these poems, we are joined to others whose lives span place and time. We discover unexpected connections in our common humanity. Topics that might not be brought up in everyday conversation can be alluded to in the metaphoric and distilled language of poetry. The late Adrienne Rich put it this way: "Wherever I turn these days, I'm looking, as from the corner of my eye, for a certain kind of poetry whose balance of dread and beauty is equal to the chaotic negations that pursue us...A complex, dialogic, coherent poetry to dissolve both complacency and despair."

A "poetry to dissolve both complacency and despair"...that is what we have tried to present in this anthology. The current clichés—*Live in the moment; Cultivate acceptance; Keep busy*—are only generalities, thin gruel all. A poem is substantial. It conveys one individual's particular experience in language. It is as much an object as a painting or a piece of music, using words as its medium. And like other art objects, it can become a precious talisman.

This last period of our lives can be many things. It can be a time of harvesting, of gathering together the various strands of our past and weaving them into a coherent fabric. It can also be a new beginning, an exploration of the unknown. We speak of "growing old." And indeed we are *growing,* growing into a new stage of life, one that can be a fulfillment of all that has come before. *To everything there is a season.* Poetry speaks to them all.

—*Mary Ann Hoberman and Carolyn Hopley, editors*

EDITORS' PREFACE

Compiling this anthology was a joyous task. We read several thousand poems to arrive at the present collection. In winnowing them down to a final number, we had to omit dozens of equally good and relevant poems, both by the poets found here and by many others. We hope this book acts as a springboard for you, the reader, to search out other poems to complement the ones we have included.

Among the criteria we used in choosing poems was the matter of accessibility. Unfortunately many potential readers are put off by modern poetry's reputation of being difficult to understand; and indeed some of it is. However, "difficult" does not mean "impossible." Some poems offer up their meanings easily; others benefit from repeated readings. But none of the poems in this book are of the variety that limit themselves to an in-group coterie.

To this point we sometimes make brief comments on a poem's form, references, and/or language. We also may note how a poem speaks to others in the collection. You will undoubtedly make further connections of your own. And while the twelve divisions of this book hold in a general way, many of the poems defied easy classification. A poem slotted under the passage of time is also about memories of childhood; one about the loss of a loved one describes in detail the natural world once shared.

We envision this book as either atop a pile on your bedside table or as the catalyst for group reading and discussion — or both. Reading poetry to oneself is one of life's great pleasures. Reading it with others can be another. For more than ten years Mary Ann has led a monthly poetry-reading group in her home, with Carolyn as a charter member. During that time we have read aloud the works of most of the poets included here. It continues to surprise us how a collaborative reading can reveal new dimensions of a poem, especially when read and spoken simultaneously.

These poems run the gamut of style and substance, from traditional to free verse, from formal to colloquial language, from serious to silly. Some of them are concerned directly with age and aging, others touch on the subject tangentially. Their authors range from Nobel laureates to the recently published; a few lived more than a thousand years ago while others are alive today. While the majority of the poems were written in English, others are presented here in translation. But all of them answer our primary criteria: they speak to us directly and honestly, and they are pertinent in some way to coming to age.

1

"YOU READING THIS, BE READY"

These first poems place us squarely in the present moment, the here and now. We spend so much of our time mulling over the past — regrets, mistakes, nostalgia — or anticipating the future that the present often escapes our attention. But realizing that the present moment is the only one we have can sharpen our awareness of what it is to be alive. Since the poet is concerned with the particular — *this* time, *this* place — a poem by example might encourage us to look at the wonder of our own situation as the gift that it is. We might call it, as Ursula K. Le Guin does, the present as a present.

YOU READING THIS, BE READY

Starting here, what do you want to remember?
How sunlight creeps along a shining floor?
What scent of old wood hovers, what softened
sound from outside fills the air?

Will you ever bring a better gift for the world
than the breathing respect that you carry
wherever you go right now? Are you waiting
for time to show you some better thoughts?

When you turn around, starting here, lift this
new glimpse that you found; carry into evening
all that you want from this day. This interval you spent
reading or hearing this, keep it for life—

What can anyone give you greater than now,
starting here, right in this room, when you turn around?

William Stafford

A GLASS OF COLD WATER

Poetry is not a code
to be broken
but a way of seeing
with the eyes shut,
of short-circuiting
the usual
connections until
lioness and
knee become
the same thing.

Though not a cure
it can console,
the way cool sheets
console
the dying flesh,
the way a glass of cold
water can be
a way station
on the unswerving
road to thirst.

Linda Pastan

This poem is placed early in the book to remind us at the outset of what a poem is and is not. It is not an enigmatic paraphrase of some secret meaning, designed to baffle and thwart the uninitiated reader. Rather, as the poet says, it is "a way of seeing...short-circuiting the usual connections."

No two readers will read a poem identically. Nor will they necessarily take away exactly what the poet intended to convey. But if a poem touches a nerve or calls up a lost memory, if one of its images pleases or some of its sounds tickle the ear, consider these as doorways into the poem.

DEW LIGHT

Now in the blessed days of more and less
when the news about time is that each day
there is less of it I know none of that
as I walk out through the early garden
only the day and I are here with no
before or after and the dew looks up
without a number or a present age

W. S. Merwin

LAMENT

Suddenly, after you die, those friends
who never agreed about anything
agree about your character.
They're like a houseful of singers rehearsing
the same score:
you were just, you were kind, you lived a fortunate life.
No harmony. No counterpoint. Except
they're not performers;
real tears are shed.

Luckily, you're dead; otherwise
you'd be overcome with revulsion.
But when that's passed,
when the guests begin filing out, wiping their eyes
because, after a day like this,
shut in with orthodoxy,
the sun's amazingly bright,
though it's late afternoon, September —
when the exodus begins,
that's when you'd feel
pangs of envy.

Your friends the living embrace one another,
gossip a little on the sidewalk
as the sun sinks, and the evening breeze
ruffles the women's shawls —
this, this, is the meaning of
"a fortunate life": it means
to exist in the present.

Louise Glück

ENOUGH

It's a gift, this cloudless November morning
warm enough for you to walk without a jacket
along your favorite path. The rhythmic shushing
of your feet through the fallen leaves should be
enough to quiet the mind, so it surprises you
when you catch yourself telling off the boss
for a decade of accumulated injustices,
all the things you've never said circling inside you.

It's the rising wind that pulls you out of it,
and you look up to see a cloud of leaves
swirling in sunlight, flickering against the blue
and rising above the treetops, as if the whole day
were sighing, *Let it go, let it go,*
for this moment at least, let it all go.

Jeffrey Harrison

MY BIRTHDAY PRESENT

Seventy-nine, seventy-nine,
I say it over, and every time
it sounds peculiar. Is it a prime?
It's a queer number, seventy-nine.
I will enter my eightieth year
tomorrow evening, somewhere near
six o'clock, around dinnertime,
my mother told me. That's a queer
hour to be born, or to enter an eightieth year.
But all of it's queer, being here.
Thinking how what I thought was mine
was only borrowed, and what was dear
has been forgotten, and every line
I've written will become a sign
for nothing at all, given time.
But that's what I was given, time.
That's my present, present time.

Ursula K. Le Guin

THE DECISION

There is a moment before a shape
hardens, a color sets.
Before the fixative or heat of kiln.
The letter might still be taken
from the mailbox.
The hand held back by the elbow,
the word kept between the larynx pulse
and the amplifying drum-skin of the room's air.
The thorax of an ant is not as narrow.
The green coat on old copper weighs more.
Yet something slips through it—
looks around,
sets out in the new direction, for other lands.
Not into exile, not into hope. Simply changed.
As a sandy track-rut changes when called a Silk Road:
it cannot be after turned back from.

Jane Hirshfield

What is a moment in time? Can it be measured? In a striking series of visual and aural comparisons, Hirshfield gradually compresses time to the narrowest possible dimension, thereby demonstrating how an apparently inconsequential decision may have momentous results. All in her journey to the awkward but inevitable last line.

THE ROUND

Light splashed this morning
on the shell-pink anemones
swaying on their tall stems;
down blue-spiked veronica
light flowed in rivulets
over the humps of the honeybees;
this morning I saw light kiss
the silk of the roses
in their second flowering,
my late bloomers
flushed with their brandy.
A curious gladness shook me.

So I have shut the doors of my house,
so I have trudged downstairs to my cell,
so I am sitting in semi-dark
hunched over my desk
with nothing for a view
to tempt me
but a bloated compost heap
steamy old stinkpile,
under my window;
and I pick my notebook up
and I start to read aloud
the still-wet words I scribbled
on the blotted page:
"Light splashed..."

I can scarcely wait till tomorrow
when a new life begins for me,
as it does each day,
as it does each day.

Stanley Kunitz

2

"THE SOUND OF TIME"

We experience the passage of time in many ways. It can both speed up and slow down, sometimes almost simultaneously. Minutes can feel like hours (a watched pot never boils) and vice versa (so-called "flow"). The summers of childhood are endless; those of old age vanish in a twinkling. But one thing is certain: the less time we have ahead of us, the more importance it assumes.

As we relinquish various activities and undergo inevitable losses, our thoughts about time change. Perhaps for the first time, life's finitude becomes real. And many poets whose youthful work has been considered obscure start to write more openly and directly as they face the end of their lives. There is a new, more common ground between author and audience. But the mystery of time remains for all of us.

> Time present and time past
> Are both perhaps present in time future,
> And time future contained in time past.
> *T. S. Eliot, from "Burnt Norton"*

FALL WIND

Pods of summer crowd around the door;
I take them in the autumn of my hands.

Last night I heard the first cold wind outside;
the wind blew soft, and yet I shiver twice:

Once for the thin walls, once for the sound of time.

William Stafford

SLOW SEASON

Now light is less; noon skies are wide and deep;
The ravages of wind and rain are healed.
The haze of harvest drifts along the field
Until clear eyes put on the look of sleep.

The garden spider weaves a silken pear
To keep inclement weather from its young.
Straight from the oak, the gossamer is hung.
At dusk our slow breath thickens on the air.

Lost hues of birds the trees take as their own.
Long since, bronze wheat was gathered into sheaves.
The walker trudges ankle-deep in leaves;
The feather of the milkweed flutters down.

The shoots of spring have mellowed with the year.
Buds, long unsealed, obscure the narrow lane.
The blood slows trance-like in the altered vein;
Our vernal wisdom moves through ripe to sere.

Theodore Roethke

Here the poet takes one of the most commonplace of comparisons — that between the year's aging and our own — and, by his virtuosic choice of language and cadence, fashions an exquisite lyric poem. Read it aloud, slowly, savoring both sense and sound.

SEASON TO SEASON

I have been fooled before, and just because
This summer seems so long, it might not be
My last. Winter could come again, and pause
The sky liked a taped tactical descent
Of pocket paratroopers. Things to see
Could happen yet, and life prove not quite spent
But still abundant, still the main event.

The trick, I'm learning, is to stay in doubt,
Season to season, of what time might bring,
And patiently await how things turn out.
Eventually time tells you everything.
If it takes time to do so, no surprise
In that. You fold your arms, you scan the skies,
And tell yourself that life has made you wise,

If only by the way it ebbs away.
But still it takes an age, and after all,
Though nearly gone, life didn't end today,
And you might be here when the first leaves fall
Or even when the snow begins again,
If life that cast you, when this all began,
As a small boy, still needs a dying man.

Clive James

LONG LIFE

Late Summer. Sunshine. The eucalyptus tree.
    It is a fortune beyond any deserving
to be still *here*, with no more than everyday worries,
    placidly arranging lines of poetry.

I consider a stick of cinnamon
    bound in raffia, finches
in the grass, and a stubby bush
    which this year mothered a lemon.

These days I speak less of death
    than the mysteries of survival. I am
no longer lonely, not yet frail, and
    after surgery, recognize each breath

as a miracle. My generation may not be
    nimble but, forgive us,
we'd like to hold on, stubbornly
    content — even while ageing.

Elaine Feinstein

While giving thanks for the miracle of daily life, the speaker is also offering a sardonic challenge to some current attitudes toward the old.

THE WAY IT IS

There's a thread you follow. It goes among
things that change. But it doesn't change.
People wonder about what you are pursuing.
You have to explain about the thread.
But it is hard for others to see.
While you hold it you can't get lost.
Tragedies happen: people get hurt
or die; and you suffer and get old.
Nothing you do can stop time's unfolding.
You don't ever let go of the thread.

William Stafford

STARFISH

This is what life does. It lets you walk up to
the store to buy breakfast and the paper, on a
stiff knee. It lets you choose the way you have
your eggs, your coffee. Then it sits a fisherman
down beside you at the counter who says, *Last night
the channel was full of starfish.* And you wonder,
is this a message, finally, or just another day?

Life lets you take the dog for a walk down to the
pond, where whole generations of biological
processes are boiling beneath the mud. Reeds
speak to you of the natural world: they whisper,
they sing. And herons pass by. Are you old
enough to appreciate the moment? Too old?
There is movement beneath the water, but it
may be nothing. There may be nothing going on.

And then life suggests that you remember the
years you ran around, the years you developed
a shocking lifestyle, advocated careless abandon,
owned a chilly heart. Upon reflection, you are
genuinely surprised to find how quiet you have
become. And then life lets you go home to think
about all this. Which you do, for quite a long time.

Later, you wake up beside your old love, the one
who never had any conditions, the one who waited
you out. This is life's way of letting you know that
you are lucky. (It won't give you *smart* or *brave,*
so you'll have to settle for lucky.) Because you
were born at a good time. Because you were able
to listen when people spoke to you. Because you
stopped when you should have and started again.

So life lets you have a sandwich, and pie for your
late night dessert. (Pie for the dog as well.) And
then life sends you back to bed, to dreamland,
while outside, the starfish drift through the channel,
with smiles on their starry faces as they head
out to deep water, to the far and boundless sea.

Eleanor Lerman

ALICE AT ONE HUNDRED AND TWO

Yes, she said, I want to live a lot more years
and see what happens, but

I want new fruits—a century of apples, oranges
and bananas is enough.

And I want new rooms. I want balustrades,
inglenooks, casement windows, and chintz!
Yes, I want chintz! Whatever happened to chintz,
with the sunlight or lamplight carving mother,
grandmother, aunt, out of its shadows?

And I want something to happen here, quickly—
the inexplicable death of a wealthy tycoon, six
likely suspects—midnight melodrama, love and
betrayal—a diamond robbery, fugitive in disguise—
a great-grandson eloping with a dancer from New Orleans.
Something!

Yes, she said, I want to live a lot more years,
but not so slowly.

Elizabeth Alexander

POSTHUMOUS LETTER TO GILBERT WHITE

It's rather sad we can only meet people
whose dates overlap with ours, a real shame that
you and Thoreau (we know that he read you)
never shook hands. He was, we hear, a rabid

Anti-Clerical and quick-tempered, you the
quietest of curates, yet I think he might well have
found in you the Ideal Friend he wrote of
with such gusto, but never ran into.

Stationaries, both of you, but keen walkers,
chaste by nature and, it would seem, immune to
the beck of worldly power, kin spirits,
who found all creatures amusive, even

the tortoise in spite of its joyless stupors,
aspected the vagrant moods of the Weather,
from the modest conduct of fogs to
the coarse belch of thunder of the rainbow's

federal arch, what fun you'd have had surveying
two rival landscapes and their migrants, noting
the pitches owls hoot on, comparing
the echo-response of dactyls and spondees.

Selfishly, I, too, would have plumbed to know you:
I could have learned so much. I'm apt to fancy
myself as a lover of Nature,
but have no right to, really. How many

birds and plants can I spot? At most two dozen.
You might, though, have found such an ignoramus
a pesky bore. Time spared you that: I
have, though, thank God, the right to re-read you.

W. H. Auden

ARS POETICA

To gaze at the river made of time and water
And recall that time itself is another river,
To know we cease to be, just like the river,
And that our faces pass away, just like the water.

To feel that waking is another sleep
That dreams it does not sleep and that death,
Which our flesh dreads, is that very death
Of every night, which we call sleep.

To see in the day or in the year a symbol
Of mankind's days and of his years,
To transform the outrage of the years
Into a music, a rumor and a symbol,

To see in death a sleep, and in the sunset
A sad gold, of such is Poetry
Immortal and a pauper. For Poetry
Returns like the dawn and the sunset.

At times in the afternoons a face
Looks at us from the depths of a mirror;
Art must be like that mirror
That reveals to us this face of ours.

They tell how Ulysses, glutted with wonders,
Wept with love to descry his Ithaca
Humble and green. Art is that Ithaca
Of green eternity, not of wonders.

It is also like an endless river
That passes and remains, a mirror for one same
Inconstant Heraclitus, who is the same
And another, like an endless river.

Jorge Luis Borges
(translated from the Spanish by
Mildred Boyer and Harold Morland)

"Ars Poetica," or "The Art of Poetry," is a poem by the ancient Roman poet Horace. Other poets down through the ages have used this title for their own poems defining poetry, as Borges does here. In Horace's view poetry was an *ars*, which also means "craft" in Latin. Following this idea, Borges likens it not to a place of wonders but to the humble island of Ithaca, home of Ulysses, the hero of Homer's Greek epic the *Odyssey*. (Ulysses is the Latin version of the name Odysseus.) After leading the Greeks to victory in the Trojan War, Ulysses wandered for ten years before finally returning to the little green island that held first place in his heart.

Heraclitus, Greek philosopher of the fifth and sixth centuries BC, said famously: "No man ever steps into the same river twice, for it is not the same river and he is not the same man."

ITHACA

As you set out for Ithaca
hope the voyage is a long one,
full of adventure, full of discovery.
The Laestrygones and the Cyclopes
and angry Poseidon, do not fear them:
such on your way, you shall never meet
if your thoughts are lofty, if a noble
emotion touch your mind, your body.
The Laestrygones and Cyclopes
and angry Poseidon you shall not meet
if you carry them not in your soul,
if your soul sets them not up before you.

Hope the voyage is a long one.
May there be many a summer morning when,
with what pleasure, what joy,
you come into harbors seen for the first time:
may you stop at Phoenician bazaars
and acquire the fine things sold there,
mother of pearl and coral, amber and ebony,
sensual perfume of every kind—
as many sensual perfumes as you can.
To many Egyptian cities may you go
so you may learn, and go on learning, from their sages.

Always keep Ithaca in your mind:
to reach her is your destiny.
But do not rush your journey.
Better that it last for many years;
better to reach the island's shores in old age,
enriched by all you've obtained along the way,
not expecting Ithaca to make you wealthy.

Ithaca gave you the marvelous journey.
Without her you would not have set out.
But she has no more to give you.

And if you find her poor, Ithaca did not deceive you.
Wise as you will have become, so full of experience,
you will have understood by then what these Ithacas mean.

C. P. *Cavafy*
*(compilation of various English translations
by the editors)*

In this poem Ulysses's voyage is once more a metaphor for the journey of life. Even though modern poets have for the most part renounced the formal conventions of poetry in favor of a less restrictive style, they often reference classical sources in their work, as Cavafy does here.

The Laestrygones and Cyclopes were mythological tribes of giant cannibals who attacked Odysseus and his men as they sailed back to Ithaca. Poseidon, ill-tempered god of the sea, was the father of Polyphemus, the one-eyed Cyclops who devoured two of Odysseus's men.

IMMIGRATION LAW

When I ask the experts
"how much time do I have?"
I don't want an answer
in years or arguments.

I must know
if there are hours enough
to mend this relationship,
see a book all the way to its birthing,
stand beside my father
on his journey.

I want to know how many seasons of chamisa
will be yellow then grey-green
and yellow
          /light/
                again,
how many red cactus flowers
will bloom beside my door.

I will not follow language
like a dog with its tail between its legs.

I need time equated with music,
hours rising in bread,
years deep from connections.

The present always holds a tremor of the past.

Give me a handful of future
to rub against my lips.

Margaret Randall

Chamisa is an aster, sometimes blooming twice in a season.

3

"THE GRACE OF THE WORLD"

When we speak of Nature, it is often as something separate from us. But even the slightest reflection reminds us that we, too, are part of the natural world, and we cut ourselves off from it at our peril. Especially in this time of rapid technological change, which leaves many of us panting at the sidelines, "the peace of wild things" becomes ever more precious, while the consequences of our actions vis-à-vis our environment grow more and more disturbing.

Poets, too, look to Nature for solace, and take refuge in the beauty of the visible world. They delight in the smallest details — a single leaf, a slant of sunlight — as well as the majesty of the heavens and the radiance of the stars. But they also imagine Nature looking back at us with sorrow — or taking no notice of us at all.

SUNDAY MORNING (*EXCERPT*)

What is divinity if it can come
Only in silent shadows and in dreams?
Shall she not find in comforts of the sun,
In pungent fruit and bright, green wings, or else
In any balm or beauty of the earth
Things to be cherished like the thought of heaven?
Divinity must live within herself:
Passions of rain, or moods in falling snow;
Grievings in loneliness, or unsubdued
Elations when the forest blooms; gusty
Emotions on wet roads on autumn nights;
All pleasures and all pains, remembering
The bough of summer and the winter branch.
These are the measures destined for her soul.

Wallace Stevens

Here, in this portion of a stanza from a much longer poem, a woman questions traditional religious beliefs passed on to her by those no longer alive. Should not divinity encompass the entire natural world and everything that exists, both dark and light? To read the complete poem is to grapple with Stevens's complex views about life and death and the nature of heaven.

BRIDGE

Most of my life was spent
building a bridge out over the sea
though the sea was too wide.
I'm proud of the bridge
hanging in the pure sea air. Machado
came for a visit and we sat on the
end of the bridge, which was his idea.

Now that I'm old, the work goes slowly.
Ever nearer death, I like it out here
high above the sea bundled
up for the arctic storms of late fall,
the resounding crash and moan of the sea,
the hundred-foot depth of the green troughs.
Sometimes the sea roars and howls like
the animal it is, a continent wide and alive.
What beauty in this the darkest music
over which you can hear the lightest music of human
behavior, the tender connection between men and galaxies.

So I sit on the edge, wagging my feet above
the abyss. Tonight the moon will be in my lap.
This is my job, to study the universe
from my bridge. I have the sky, the sea, the faint
green streak of Canadian forest on the far shore.

Jim Harrison

Since Antonio Machado, one of Spain's greatest poets, died in 1939 and Harrison was born in 1939, we have to assume that Machado's visit was imaginary. What is the bridge?

THE PEACE OF WILD THINGS

When despair for the world grows in me
and I wake in the night at the least sound
in fear of what my life and my children's lives may be,
I go and lie down where the wood drake
rests in his beauty on the water, and the great heron feeds.
I come into the peace of wild things
who do not tax their lives with forethought
of grief. I come into the presence of still water.
And I feel above me the day-blind stars
waiting with their light. For a time
I rest in the grace of the world, and am free.

Wendell Berry

NIGHT ON THE PRAIRIES

Night on the prairies,
The supper is over, the fire on the ground burns low,
The wearied emigrants sleep, wrapt in their blankets;
I walk by myself—I stand and look at the stars, which I think now
    I never realized before.

Now I absorb immortality and peace,
I admire death and test propositions.

How plenteous! how spiritual! how resumé!
The same old man and soul—the same old aspirations, and the
    same content.

I was thinking the day most splendid till I saw what the not-day
    exhibited,
I was thinking this globe enough till there sprang out so noiseless
    around me myriads of other globes.

Now while the great thoughts of space and eternity fill me I will
    measure myself by them,
And now touch'd with the lives of other globes arrived as far
    along as those of the earth,
Or waiting to arrive, or pass'd on farther than those of earth,
I henceforth no more ignore them than I ignore my own life,
Or the lives of the earth arrived as far as mine, or waiting to
    arrive.

O I see now that life cannot exhibit all to me, as the day cannot,
I see that I am to wait for what will be exhibited by death.

Walt Whitman

Walt Whitman wrote this poem when he was forty-one, thirty-two years before his death. It is eerily prescient of our contemporary concerns, as is so much of his poetry.

"Resumé" in this nineteenth-century usage means "resumed," the past participle (used as a noun) of the French verb *"résumer."*

TO AN EASTERN BLUEBIRD

You beak-chattering blaze of blue,
patch of sky squatting on a power line,
teach me to cock my head, too.

Together, we'll watch — what *is* there to see
in Tennessee? July can only shrug,
after a night's caterwaul of katydids.

Now, in the deserted street, a fawn tiptoes
from the woods toward well-tamed lawn.
A dead branch moves, doe rustling to life.

You keep singing, bird, and no one minds,
but I have drawn breath too noisily —
toward me, eyes carved of obsidian turn.

Into mossy ears as big as a man's cupped hand
a clamor pours: somewhere beneath us,
a mole shoves earth from one dark to another.

Blood blunders through the chambers of my heart.
My life waits to turn the page from fifty-nine to sixty.
A feather too blue to be real — how long does it last?

Debora Greger

A LEAF

A leaf, one of the last, parts from a maple branch:
it is spinning in the transparent air of October, falls
on a heap of others, stops, fades. No one
admired its entrancing struggle with the wind,
followed its flight, no one will distinguish it now
as it lies among other leaves, no one saw
what I did. I am
the only one.

Bronislaw Maj
(translated from the Polish by
Czeslaw Milosz)

BINSEY POPLARS

felled 1879

My aspens dear, whose airy cages quelled,
  Quelled or quenched in leaves the leaping sun,
  All felled, felled, are all felled;
   Of a fresh and following folded rank
        Not spared, not one
        That dandled a sandalled
     Shadow that swam or sank
On meadow & river & wind-wandering weed-winding bank.

 O if we but knew what we do
    When we delve or hew —
   Hack and rack the growing green!
     Since country is so tender
   To touch, her being so slender,
   That, like this sleek and seeing ball
   But a prick will make no eye at all,
   Where we, even where we mean
      To mend her we end her,
    When we hew or delve:
After-comers cannot guess the beauty been.
  Ten or twelve, only ten or twelve

Strokes of havoc unselve
    The sweet especial scene,
Rural scene, a rural scene,
Sweet especial rural scene.

Gerard Manley Hopkins

Almost one hundred fifty years ago Hopkins was bewailing the destruction of his beloved trees in a style that has never quite been replicated. It harks back to Old English or Anglo-Saxon, which in turn comes from the ancient Teutonic. Using a vocabulary that eschews most words of Latin origin, he relies on the alliteration and repetition of one-syllable words, placing great emphasis on their sound while at the same time keeping them anchored to their specific meanings.

The effects of the destruction both on the land and on our spirits resonate deeply with our contemporary concerns.

THREAT

You can live for years next door
to a big pinetree, honored to have
so venerable a neighbor, even
when it sheds needles all over your flowers
or wakes you, dropping big cones
onto your deck at still of night.
Only when, before dawn one year
at the vernal equinox, the wind
rises and rises, raising images
of cockleshell boats tossed among huge
advancing walls of waves,
do you become aware that always,
under respect, under your faith
in the pinetree's beauty, there lies
the fear it will crash some day
down on your house, on you in your bed,
on the fragility of the safe
dailiness you have almost
grown used to.

Denise Levertov

AN OLD-FASHIONED SONG

(Nous n'irons plus au bois)

No more walks in the wood:
The trees have all been cut
Down, and where once they stood
Not even a wagon rut
Appears along the path
Low brush is taking over.

No more walks in the wood;
This is the aftermath
Of afternoons in the clover
Fields where we once made love
Then wandered home together
Where the trees arched above,
Where we made our own weather
When branches were the sky.
Now they are gone for good,
And you, for ill, and I
Am only a passer-by.

We and the trees and the way
Back from the fields of play
Lasted as long as we could.
No more walks in the wood.

John Hollander

SPECIES

For seasons beyond count, age
after age, through generations,
they watched us, naked of eye,

through every possible lens:
we were pictured, widely, as
of more or less intelligence.

They measured our migrations,
guessed at the code in our blood,
the tidal pull of the sun,

or what the stars told us.
In weather when we spoke clearly
what they only partially sensed,

they knew to tape our voices;
they collected how they thought
we spoke. Or sang. Of how

we spoke they wrote music.
To our habitats, fieldmarks, even
our habits of pairing, they made

themselves guides. They saw
in us an endangered species;
they listed us with governments.

Out of guilt for the hunting,
even long after, or for what
we barely reminded them of,

we believe they almost loved us.
What we can never know is
how we failed to let them feel

what we meant in our deepest instinct,
in the great dance of our silence.
At the latitudes where we winter,

we only know to gather, to sing
to our young and ourselves, warning
after warning of how they became extinct.

Philip Booth

REQUIEM

The crucified planet Earth,
should it find a voice
and a sense of irony,
might now well say
of our abuse of it,
"Forgive them, Father,
they know not what they do."

The irony would be
that we know what
we are doing.

When the last living thing
has died on account of us,
how poetical it would be
if Earth could say,
in a voice floating up
perhaps
from the floor
of the Grand Canyon,
"It is done."
People did not like it here.

Kurt Vonnegut

GRAVELLY RUN

I don't know somehow it seems sufficient
to see and hear whatever coming and going is,
losing the self to the victory
    of stones and trees,
of bending sandpit lakes, crescent
round groves of dwarf pine:

for it is not so much to know the self
as to know it as it is known
    by galaxy and cedar cone,
as if birth had never found it
and death could never end it:

the swamp's slow water comes
down Gravelly Run fanning the long
    stone-held algal
hair and narrowing roils between
the shoulders of the highway bridge:

holly grows on the banks in the woods there,
and the cedars' gothic-clustered
    spires could make
green religion in winter bones:

so I look and reflect, but the air's glass
jail seals each thing in its entity:

no use to make any philosophies here:
    I see no
god in the holly, hear no song from
the snowbroken weeds: Hegel is not the winter

yellow in the pines: the sunlight has never
heard of trees: surrendered self among
   unwelcoming forms: stranger,
hoist your burdens, get on down the road.

A. R. Ammons

Here the stoic speaker postulates a bleak division between humanity and the rest of nature as well as the separation of each natural entity from all the others. He claims this existentialist view "seems sufficient." Who is the "stranger" he addresses?

Georg Wilhelm Friedrich Hegel was an early-nineteenth-century German idealist philosopher.

WINTER PARADISE

Now I am old and free from time
How spacious life,
Unbeginning unending sky where the wind blows
The ever-moving clouds and clouds of starlings on the wing.
Chaffinch and apple-leaf across my garden lawn,
Winter paradise
With its own birds and daisies
And all the near and far that eye can see
Each blade of grass signed with the mystery
Across whose face unchanging and everchanging pass
Summer and winter, day and night.
Great countenance of the unknown known
You have looked upon me all my days,
More loved than lover's face,
More merciful than the heart, more wise
Than spoken word, unspoken theme
Simple as earth in whom we live and move.

Kathleen Raine

This poem stands in absolute contrast to the previous one. Here the natural world embraces us; we are an integral part of it. Is it possible in some way to hold both views?

PEBBLE

The pebble
is a perfect creature

equal to itself
mindful of its limits

filled exactly
with pebbly meaning

with a scent that does not remind one of anything
does not frighten anything away does not arouse desire

its ardour and coldness
are just and full of dignity

I feel a heavy remorse
when I hold it in my hand
and its noble body
is permeated by false warmth

  —Pebbles cannot be tamed
    to the end they will look at us
    with a calm and very clear eye.

Zbigniew Herbert
(translated from the Polish by
Czeslaw Milosz and Peter Dale Scott)

DUST OF SNOW

The way a crow
Shook down on me
The dust of snow
From a hemlock tree

Has given my heart
A change of mood
And saved some part
Of a day I rued.

Robert Frost

4

"BODY MY HOUSE"

We are incarnate beings, but unlike other beings, we are uniquely aware of our incarnation. And one of the most vexing puzzles of existence is the nature of the connection between our bodies and our minds. As we grow older, our bodies change; indeed they are the visible proof of our aging. Our physical abilities diminish as well. Yet inside we may feel that we are still ourselves, even a plurality of selves, from infancy through current age.

When illness attacks, the body can become an enemy or a battle-field on which a war is played out. But at the same time, frailty and illness can bring us to experience more deeply the intangible blessings of life: love, friendship, kindness. And our aging bodies may also bring this compensatory paradox: the more slowly we move in space, the more time we have to explore our immediate surroundings and our inner selves.

And if we are lucky, we can sometimes laugh at ourselves along the way.

QUESTION

Body my house
my horse my hound
what will I do
when you are fallen

Where will I sleep
How will I ride
What will I hunt

Where can I go
without my mount
all eager and quick
How will I know
in thicket ahead
is danger or treasure
when Body my good
bright dog is dead

How will it be
to lie in the sky
without roof or door
and wind for an eye

With cloud for shift
how will I hide?

May Swenson

LIVING IN THE BODY

Body is something you need in order to stay
on this planet and you only get one.
And no matter which one you get, it will not
be satisfactory. It will not be beautiful
enough, it will not be fast enough, it will
not keep on for days at a time, but will
pull you down into a sleepy swamp and
demand apples and coffee and chocolate cake.

Body is a thing you have to carry
from one day into the next. Always the
same eyebrows over the same eyes in the same
skin when you look in the mirror, and the
same creaky knee when you get up from the
floor and the same wrist under the watchband.
The changes you can make are small and
costly — better to leave it as it is.

Body is a thing that you have to leave
eventually. You know that because you have
seen others do it, others who were once like you,
living inside their pile of bones and
flesh, smiling at you, loving you,
leaning in the doorway, talking to you
for hours and then one day they
are gone. No forwarding address.

Joyce Sutphen

SUNSET FROM THE WINDOW OF A RENTED SUMMER HOUSE

They skipped, our mothers, down the path to the sea. Through wild phlox, beach plums, prickly clusters of pasture rose. Our mothers were naked. Their backs. Their buttocks—we were shooed from the window. By our fathers, who took matters in hand. It was August. Foghorn, ferry, the forking cry of gulls. Pink froth bibbed the outgoing tide. Life-listers flit across sea-bleached shells. Our fathers were husbands who kissed their wives. We pressed our noses to the glass. We were still too young to see ourselves.

Diane Louie

HERE

Here I am in the garden laughing
an old woman with heavy breasts
and a nicely mapped face

how did this happen
well that's who I wanted to be

at last a   woman
in the old style   sitting
stout thighs apart under
a big skirt   grandchild sliding
on   off my lap   a pleasant
summer perspiration

that's my old man across the yard
he's talking to the meter reader
he's telling him the world's sad story
how electricity is oil or uranium
and so forth   I tell my grandson
run over to your grandpa   ask him
to sit beside me for a minute   I
am suddenly exhausted by my desire
to kiss his sweet explaining lips

Grace Paley

LASTING

"Fish oils," my doctor snorted, "and oily fish
are actually good for you. What's actually wrong
for anyone your age are all those dishes
with thick sauce that we all pined for so long
as we were young and poor. Now we can afford
to order such things, just not to digest them;
we find what bills we've run up in the stored
plaque and fat cells of our next stress test."

My own last test scored in the top 10 percent
of males in my age bracket. Which defies
all consequences or justice — I've spent
years shackled to my desk, saved from all exercise.
My dentist, next: "Your teeth seem quite good
for someone your age, better than we'd expect
with so few checkups or cleanings. Teeth should
repay you with more grief for such neglect" —

echoing how my mother always nagged,
"Brush a full 100 strokes," and would jam
cod liver oil down our throats till we'd go gagging
off to flu-filled classrooms, crammed
with vegetables and vitamins. By now,
I've outlasted both parents whose plain food
and firm ordinance must have endowed
this heart's touch muscle — weak still in gratitude.

W. D. Snodgrass

REFUSING AT FIFTY-TWO TO WRITE SONNETS

It came to him that he could nearly count
How many Octobers he had left to him
In increments of ten or, say, eleven
Thus: sixty-three, seventy-four, eighty-five.
He couldn't see himself at ninety-six —
Humanity's advances notwithstanding
In health-care, self-help, or new-age regimens —
What with his habits and family history,
The end he thought is nearer than you think.

The future, thus confined to its contingencies,
The present moment opens like a gift:
The balding month, the grey week, the blue morning,
The hour's routine, the minute's passing glance —
All seem like godsends now. And what to make of this?
At the end the word that comes to him is Thanks.

Thomas Lynch

Definition of a sonnet: a poem with fourteen lines.

A SONG

I thought no more was needed
Youth to prolong
Than dumb-bell and foil
To keep the body young.
O who could have foretold
That the heart grows old?

Though I have many words,
What woman's satisfied,
I am no longer faint
Because at her side?
O who could have foretold
That the heart grows old?

I have not lost desire
But the heart that I had;
I thought 'twould burn my body
Laid on the death-bed,
For who could have foretold
That the heart grows old?

W. B. Yeats

Here the body and the heart are no longer synchronous. Maintaining a youthful body does not guarantee a loving heart; indeed, it may do just the opposite. Many of Yeats's poems deal with sexual appetite in age as an essential spur to his poetic creation.

MRS RIP VAN WINKLE

I sank like a stone
Into the still, deep waters
of late middle age,
Aching from head to foot.
I took up food
And gave up exercise.
It did me good.
And while he slept,
I found some hobbies
for myself.
Painting. Seeing the sights
I'd always dreamed about:
The Leaning Tower.
The Pyramids.
The Taj Mahal.
I made a little watercolour
of them all.
But what was best,
What hands-down beat
the rest,
Was saying a none-too-fond
farewell to sex.
Until the day
I came home with this
drawing of Niagara
And he was sitting up in bed
rattling Viagra.

Carol Ann Duffy

MYTH

Long afterward, Oedipus, old and blinded, walked the
roads.   He smelled a familiar smell.   It was
the Sphinx.   Oedipus said, "I want to ask one question.
Why didn't I recognize my mother?"   "You gave the
wrong answer," said the Sphinx.   "But that was what
made everything possible," said Oedipus.   "No," she said.
"When I asked, What walks on four legs in the morning,
two at noon, and three in the evening, you answered,
Man.   You didn't say anything about woman."
"When you say Man," said Oedipus, "you include women
too. Everyone knows that."   She said, "That's what
you think."

Muriel Rukeyser

MI ESTOMAGO (MY BELLY)

Naked and as if in silence
I approach my belly
it has gone on changing like summer
withdrawing from the sea
or like a dress that expands with the hours
My belly
is more than round
because when I sit down
it spreads like a brush fire
then,
I touch it to recall
all the things inside it:
salt and merriment
the fried eggs of winter breakfasts
the milk that strangled me in my youth
the Coca-Cola that stained my teeth
the nostalgia for the glass of wine
we discovered in La Isla
or french fries and olive oil
And as I remember
I feel it growing
and bowing down more and more ceremoniously to the
    ground
until it caresses my feet, my toes
that never could belong to a princess,
I rejoice
that my belly is as wide as Chepi's old sombrero—
Chepi was my grandmother—
and I pamper it no end
when it complains or has bad dreams
from eating too much.

Midsummer, at seventy years of age,
this Sunday the seventh
my belly is still with me
and proudly goes parading along the shore
some say I am already old and ugly
that my breasts are entangled with my guts
but my belly is here at my side a good companion
and don't say it's made of fat
rather tender morsels of meat toasting in the sun.

Marjorie Agosín
(translated from the Spanish by Cola Franzen)

LOSING MY TEETH

Last year a tooth dropped,
this year another one,
then six or seven went fast
and the falling is not going to stop.
All the rest are loose
and it will end when they are all gone.
I remember when I lost the first
I felt ashamed of the gap.
When two or three followed,
I worried about death.
When one is about to come loose,
I am anxious and fearful
since forked teeth are awkward with food,
and in dread I tilt my face to rinse my mouth.
Eventually it will abandon me and drop
just like a landslide.
But now the falling-out is old hat,
each tooth goes just like the others.
Fortunately I have about twenty left.
One by one they will go in order.
If one goes each year,
I have enough to last me two decades.
Actually it does not make much difference
if they go together or separately.
People say when teeth fall out
your life is fading.
I say life has its own end;
long life, short life, we all die,
with or without teeth.
They also say gaps scare

the people who see you.
I quote Zhuangzi's story —
a tree and a wild goose each has its advantages,
and though silence is better than slurring my words,
and though I can't chew, at least soft food tastes good
and I can sing out this poem
to surprise my wife and children.

Han Yu
(translated from the Chinese by Kenneth O. Hanson)

When Han Yu wrote this poem in 803, he was thirty-six years old.

CANCER AND NOVA

The star exploding in the body;
The creeping thing, growing in the brain or the bone;
The hectic cannibal, the obscene mouth.

The mouths along the meridian sought him,
Soft as moths, many a moon and sun,
Until one
In a pale fleeing dream caught him.

Waking, he did not know himself undone,
Nor walking, smiling, reading that the news was good,
The star exploding in his blood.

Hyam Plutzik

Aging is accompanied by both frailty and disease. Frailty is usually gradual:
we adjust and go on. Disease is often different. By the time it reveals itself, it
may be too late.

THE BURIAL OF THE OLD

The old, whose bodies encrust their lives,
die, and that is well.
They unhinder what has struggled in them.

The light, painfully loved, that narrowed
and darkened in their minds
becomes again the sky.

The young, who have looked on dying,
turn back to the world, grown strangely
alert to each other's bodies.

Wendell Berry

5

"THE GRAND AND DAMAGING PARADE"

Of all the losses we sustain in life, the death of someone we love is the most painful. No preparation forearms us. Even when the death is anticipated or perhaps desired, as when it is preceded by debilitating illness or dementia, we can be overwhelmed by the utter finality of the break when it comes.

Elizabeth Bishop refers to "the art of losing" and archly lists a hierarchy of losses, beginning with door keys or a wasted hour, as if small privations can prepare us for great ones. But losing those we love to Dylan Thomas's "good night" is in a category of its own. And by the time we are old, there is no way we will have escaped this experience.

Poets have treated the subject in various ways. In the past they wrote elegies, formal poems of mourning. Recently they have written in more personal terms to commemorate their losses. And while nothing can appease the first raw grief at a loved one's death, in its aftermath, poetry may offer a unique kind of solace.

THINGS SHOULDN'T BE SO HARD

A life should leave
deep tracks:
ruts where she
went out and back
to get the mail
or move the hose
around the yard;
where she used to
stand before the sink,
a worn-out place;
beneath her hand
the china knobs
rubbed down to
white pastilles;
the switch she
used to feel for
in the dark
almost erased.
Her things should
keep her marks.
The passage
of a life should show;
it should abrade.
And when life stops,
a certain space—
however small—
should be left scarred
by the grand and
damaging parade.
Things shouldn't
be so hard.

Kay Ryan

DIRGE WITHOUT MUSIC

I am not resigned to the shutting away of loving hearts in the
　　hard ground.
So it is, and so it will be, for so it has been, time out of mind:
Into the darkness they go, the wise and the lovely. Crowned
With lilies and with laurel they go; but I am not resigned.

Lovers and thinkers, into the earth with you.
Be one with the dull, the indiscriminate dust.
A fragment of what you felt, of what you knew,
A formula, a phrase remains,—but the best is lost.

The answers quick and keen, the honest look, the laughter, the
　　love,—
They are gone. They are gone to feed the roses. Elegant and
　　curled
Is the blossom. Fragrant is the blossom. I know. But I do not
　　approve.
More precious was the light in your eyes than all the roses in the
　　world.

Down, down, down into the darkness of the grave
Gently they go, the beautiful, the tender, the kind;
Quietly they go, the intelligent, the witty, the brave.
I know. But I do not approve. And I am not resigned.

Edna St. Vincent Millay

ORPHANED OLD

I feel less lucky since my parents died.
Father first, then mother, have left me
out in a downpour
roofless in cold wind
no umbrella no hood no hat no warm
native place, nothing
between me and eyeless sky.

In the gritty prevailing wind
I think of times I've carelessly lost things:
    that white-gold ring when I was eight,
    a classmate named Mercedes Williams,
    my passport in Gibraltar,
    my maiden name.

Marie Ponsot

While our parents are still alive, they somehow protect us even as we our-
selves age. With their deaths, nothing stands between us and oblivion.
Much of our loss is what they take with them — who we were as children, our
history. Their deaths bring to mind other losses, both commonplace and
profound.

IN VIEW OF THE FACT

The people of my time are passing away: my
wife is baking for a funeral, a 60-year-old who

died suddenly, when the phone rings, and it's
Ruth we care so much about in intensive care:

it was once weddings that came so thick and
fast, and then, first babies, such a hullabaloo:

now, it's this that and the other and somebody
else gone or on the brink: well, we never

thought we would live forever (although we did)
and now it looks like we won't: some of us

are losing a leg to diabetes, some don't know
what they went downstairs for, some know that

a hired watchful person is around, some like
to touch the cane tip into something steady,

so nice: we have already lost so many,
brushed the loss of ourselves ourselves: our

address books for so long a slow scramble now
are palimpsests, scribbles and scratches: our

index cards for Christmases, birthdays,
Halloweens drop clean away into sympathies:

at the same time we are getting used to so
many leaving, we are hanging on with a grip

to the ones left: we are not giving up on the
congestive heart failure or brain tumors, on

the nice old men left in empty houses or on
the widows who decide to travel a lot: we

think the sun may shine someday when we'll
drink wine together and think of what used to

be: until we die we will remember every
single thing, recall every word, love every

loss: then we will, as we must, leave it to
others to love, love that can grow brighter

and deeper till the very end, gaining strength
and getting more precious all the way....

A. R. Ammons

THE LAST THINGS

Of course there's always a last everything.
The last meal, the last drink, the last sex.
The last meeting with a friend. The last
stroking of the last cat, the last
sight of a son or daughter. Some would be more
charged with emotion than others — if one knew.
It's not knowing that makes it all so piquant.
A good many lasts have taken place already.

Then there are last words, variously reported,
such as: Don't let poor Nelly starve. Or:
I think I could eat one of Bellamy's veal pies.
If there were time I'd incline to a summary:
Alcohol made my life shorter but more interesting.
My father said (not last perhaps): Say goodbye to Gavin.

Gavin Ewart

ONE ART

The art of losing isn't hard to master;
so many things seem filled with the intent
to be lost that their loss is not disaster.

Lose something every day. Accept the fluster
of lost door keys, the hour badly spent.
The art of losing isn't hard to master.

Then practice losing farther, losing faster:
places, and names, and where it was you meant
to travel. None of these will bring disaster.

I lost my mother's watch. And look! my last, or
next-to-last, of three loved houses went.
The art of losing isn't hard to master.

I lost two cities, lovely ones. And, vaster,
some realms I owned, two rivers, a continent.
I miss them, but it wasn't a disaster.

—Even losing you (the joking voice, a gesture
I love) I shan't have lied. It's evident
the art of losing's not too hard to master
though it may look like (*Write* it!) like disaster.

Elizabeth Bishop

This poem is a villanelle, an originally French form of verse consisting of five three-line stanzas, or tercets, and one concluding four-line stanza, or quatrain. The nineteen-line poem uses only two rhymes; the first and third lines of the first stanza alternate as refrains in the following stanzas and are repeated as the final two lines of the poem.

Obviously this poetic form is complicated and presents a real challenge to its author. But when it works, as here, the repetitions and subtle variations of rhyme and meaning and the escalation of emotion make it both powerful and memorable.

DO NOT GO GENTLE INTO THAT GOOD NIGHT

Do not go gentle into that good night,
Old age should burn and rage at close of day;
Rage, rage against the dying of the light.

Though wise men at their end know dark is right,
Because their words had forked no lightning they
Do not go gentle into that good night.

Good men, the last wave by, crying how bright
Their frail deeds might have danced in a green bay
Rage, rage against the dying of the light.

Wild men who caught and sang the sun in flight,
And learn, too late, they grieved it on its way,
Do not go gentle into that good night.

Grave men, near death, who see with blinding sight
Blind eyes could blaze like meteors and be gay,
Rage, rage against the dying of the light.

And you, my father, there on that sad height,
Curse, bless, me now with your fierce tears, I pray.
Do not go gentle into that good night.
Rage, rage against the dying of the light.

Dylan Thomas

Like the previous poem, this, too, is a villanelle. At first hearing, preferably as recited by Thomas himself, the listener is carried away by its hypnotic intricacy.

THOSE – DYING THEN

Those – dying then,
Knew where they went –
They went to God's Right Hand –
That Hand is amputated now
And God cannot be found –

The abdication of Belief
Makes the Behavior small –
Better an ignis fatuus
Than no illume at all –

Emily Dickinson

"Ignis fatuus," a Latin phrase, literally translates as "foolish fire." It is used in the sense of "will-o'-the-wisp" — something deluding or deceptive. A will-o'-the-wisp is a ghostly light sometimes seen over marshes that recedes as travelers approach it and leads them to stray off their path. This painful conflict between lack of and hunger for religious belief pervades many of Dickinson's poems.

EXCEPT

Now that you have gone
and I am alone and quiet,
my contentment would be
complete, if I did not wish
you were here so I could say,
"How good it is, Tanya,
to be alone and quiet."

Wendell Berry

MARY NO MORE

Yesterday, the day you died,
Was dark and wet. The sky wept.
It was easy to leave such a miserable place,
Damp and cold, the woods almost black at noon.

But today! O Mary
The world is washed clean and bright;
The air is clear and fresh;
The sun falls in pools of light on the lawn;
Everything is new again, restored to health.
Look, if you had lived,
At what you would see!

I think you are still here,
Looking through my eyes
At what you have left,
Calling on me to attend to it,
To all of it in your absence.

Mary Ann Hoberman

I wrote this poem when I was in my thirties. Mary was a neighbor, the mother of three friends of my three children. It was the first time I experienced the death of a contemporary who was also a wife and mother, and I felt it very deeply. Coincidentally fifty years later, one of my dearest friends, also named Mary, died on a dark, rainy day. I was with her at the time of her death, and at that very moment the sun appeared. I read this poem at her memorial.

FATHER

May 19, 1999

Today you would be ninety-seven
if you had lived, and we would all be
miserable, you and your children,
driving from clinic to clinic,
an ancient, fearful hypochondriac
and his fretful son and daughter,
asking directions, trying to read
the complicated, fading map of cures.
But with your dignity intact
you have been gone for twenty years,
and I am glad for all of us, although
I miss you every day — the heartbeat
under your necktie, the hand cupped
on the back of my neck, Old Spice
in the air, your voice delighted with stories.
On this day each year you loved to relate
that at the moment of your birth
your mother glanced out the window
and saw lilacs in bloom. Well, today
lilacs are blooming in side yards
all over Iowa, still welcoming you.

Ted Kooser

The conflict between the wish to prolong an ailing loved one's life as long as possible and the misery too often attendant on such a prolongation is a familiar one. Here the son imagines the scenario had his father gone on living and is grateful that it did not play out. Instead, he can rejoice in the memories of his father each year as the lilacs bloom again on his birthday.

CLEARANCES (*EXCERPT*)

in memoriam M.K.H., 1911–1984

When all the others were away at Mass
I was all hers as we peeled potatoes.
They broke the silence, let fall one by one
Like solder weeping off the soldering iron:
Cold comforts set between us, things to share
Gleaming in a bucket of clean water.
And again let fall. Little pleasant splashes
From each other's work would bring us to our senses.

So while the parish priest at her bedside
Went hammer and tongs at the prayers for the dying
And some were responding and some crying
I remembered her head bent towards my head,
Her breath in mine, our fluent dipping knives—
Never closer the whole rest of our lives.

Seamus Heaney

This memory of quiet intimacy between mother and son, sharing a familiar and homely household task, is contrasted with the bombast of formulaic prayer and behavior at her bedside as she lay dying.

OH ANTIC GOD

oh antic God
return to me
my mother in her thirties
leaned across the front porch
the huge pillow of her breasts
pressing against the rail
summoning me in for bed.

I am almost the dead woman's age times two.

I can barely recall her song
the scent of her hands
though her wild hair scratches my dreams
at night.   return to me, oh Lord of then
and now, my mother's calling,
her young voice humming my name.

Lucille Clifton

An arbitrary God is here called to account for acting in inexplicable ways.
"Antic," as originally defined, meant "grotesque" or "bizarre."

PARTING WITH A VIEW

I don't reproach the spring
for starting up again.
I can't blame it
for doing what it must
year after year.

I know that my grief
will not stop the green.
The grass blade may bend
but only in the wind.

It doesn't pain me to see
that clumps of alders above the water
have something to rustle with again.

I take note of the fact
that the shore of a certain lake
is still—as if you were living—
as lovely as before.

I don't resent
the view for its vista
of a sun-dazzled bay.

I am even able to imagine
some not-us
sitting at this minute
on a fallen birch trunk.

I respect their right
to whisper, laugh,
and lapse into happy silence.

I can even allow
that they are bound by love
and that he holds her
with a living arm.

Something freshly birdish
starts rustling in the reeds.
I sincerely want them
to hear it.

I don't require changes
from the surf,
now diligent, now sluggish,
obeying not me.

I expect nothing
from the depths near the woods,
first emerald,
then sapphire,
then black.

There's one thing I won't agree to:
my own return.
The privilege of presence—
I give it up.

I survived you by enough,
and only by enough,
to contemplate from afar.

Wislawa Szymborska
(translated from the Polish by
Stanislaw Baranczak and Clare Cavanagh)

"GOOD NIGHT, WILLIE LEE, I'LL SEE YOU IN THE MORNING"

Looking down into my father's
dead face
for the last time
my mother said without
tears, without smiles
without regrets
but with *civility*
"Good night, Willie Lee, I'll see you
in the morning."
And it was then I knew that the healing
of all our wounds
is forgiveness
that permits a promise
of our return
at the end.

Alice Walker

The apparent simplicity of this brief poem belies its hard-earned wisdom about death and forgiveness.

6

"INTIMATIONS OF MORTALITY"

If we are lucky enough to live a long life, youth and age are at the opposite ends of a continuum. When we are young, age is a foreign country, one we expect to visit but not for a long time. And when we eventually arrive there, we see that even if we did give it some thought, most of our speculations were off the mark.

Focusing only on our fear of death may prevent us from realizing the positive aspects of this last period of life. In our youth-centered culture, age is considered a negative: whatever wisdom it may offer cannot compensate for the physical and mental losses we sustain. In Western society this is the common viewpoint. But it is not the only one; and it need not be the one we choose to abide by.

The last years are as much a part of life as the first ones and can be equally meaningful. And while youth cannot know what it is to be old, the opposite does not hold true. It is only in old age that the whole of life becomes visible and may be seen in its entirety. Why ignore this precious gift of perspective?

> The afternoon of life is just as full of meaning as the morning;
> only, its meaning and purpose are different.
>
> *Carl Jung*

FINALLY

(in memory of Theo Moszynski)

This is what I tell myself: you are gone
On a journey, somewhere far away, perhaps
China, somewhere where they love small children,
Somewhere calm and warm, and golden
Like you, smiling, somewhere you are loved
The way you were here with us, the way
You still are. And I tell myself you are young
Forever, never growing older, never growing
Old, forever the perfectly beautiful, perfectly
Trusting child forever and ever the way I say
Sometimes I want to stop time and have a moment
Last forever, never changing, knowing it
Impossible, knowing it cannot but
Knowing now with you it is possible, you will not
Ever change and knowing finally
That is the sorrow
The true sorrow
Of death.

Mary Ann Hoberman

I wrote this poem shortly after the death of my four-year-old grandson. At the time I did not think of it as a poem but as an outpouring of grief, written in a few minutes. It was only much later when I reread it and heard it as a poem that I copied it over with the line breaks and punctuation you see above.

FEAR OF DEATH

What is it now with me
And is it as I have become?
Is there no state free from the boundary lines
Of before and after? The window is open today

And the air pours in with piano notes
In its skirts, as though to say, "Look, John,
I've brought along these and these" — that is,
A few Beethovens, some Brahmses,

A few choice Poulenc notes.... Yes,
It is being free again, the air, it has to keep coming back
Because that's all it's good for.
I want to stay with it out of fear

That keeps me from walking up certain steps,
Knocking at certain doors, fear of growing old
Alone, and of finding no one at the evening end
Of the path except another myself

Nodding a curt greeting: "Well, you've been awhile
But now we're back together, which is what counts."
Air in my path, you could shorten this,
But the breeze has dropped, and silence is the last word.

John Ashbery

Ashbery's poems are often somewhat enigmatic, and this one is no exception; but at the same time he confronts the primal fear of death head-on. Music may temper this fear but only briefly. The poem ends paradoxically in true Ashbery style: "silence is the last word."

AUBADE

I work all day, and get half-drunk at night.
Waking at four to soundless dark, I stare.
In time the curtain-edges will grow light.
Till then I see what's really always there:
Unresting death, a whole day nearer now,
Making all thought impossible but how
And where and when I shall myself die.
Arid interrogation: yet the dread
Of dying, and being dead,
Flashes afresh to hold and horrify.

The mind blanks at the glare. Not in remorse
— The good not done, the love not given, time
Torn off unused — nor wretchedly because
An only life can take so long to climb
Clear of its wrong beginnings, and may never;
But at the total emptiness for ever,
The sure extinction that we travel to
And shall be lost in always. Not to be here,
Not to be anywhere,
And soon; nothing more terrible, nothing more true.

This is a special way of being afraid
No trick dispels. Religion used to try,
That vast moth-eaten musical brocade
Created to pretend we never die,
And specious stuff that says *No rational being*
Can fear a thing it will not feel, not seeing
That this is what we fear — no sight, no sound,
No touch or taste or smell, nothing to think with,
Nothing to love or link with,
The anaesthetic from which none come round.

And so it stays just on the edge of vision,
A small unfocused blue, a standing chill
That slows each impulse down to indecision.
Most things will never happen: this one will,
And realisation of it rages out
In furnace-fear when we are caught without
People or drink. Courage is no good:
It means not scaring others. Being brave
Lets no one off the grave.
Death is no different whined at than withstood.

Slowly light strengthens, and the room takes shape.
It stands plain as a wardrobe, what we know,
Have always known, know that we can't escape,
Yet can't accept. One side will have to go.
Meanwhile telephones crouch, getting ready to ring
In locked-up offices, and all the uncaring
Intricate rented world begins to rouse.
The sky is white as clay, with no sun.
Work has to be done.
Postmen like doctors go from house to house.

Philip Larkin

An aubade is a poem or song of morning, welcoming or lamenting the dawn of day. Larkin's aubade is very definitely the latter. Here he goes through the litany of ways humanity has tried to obliterate the terror of eternal emptiness, all to no avail. But life must go on: "work has to be done," exemplified by the dependable postman and the healing doctor, making their daily rounds.

AS BEFITS A MAN

I don't mind dying—
But I'd hate to die all alone!
I want a dozen pretty women
To holler, cry, and moan!

I don't mind dying
But I want my funeral to be fine:
A row of long tall mamas
Fainting, fanning, and crying.

I want a fish-tail hearse
And sixteen fish-tail cars,
A big brass band
And a whole truck load of flowers.

When they let me down,
Down into the clay,
I want the women to holler:
Please don't take him away!
    Ow-ooo-oo-o!
Don't take daddy away!

                                    Langston Hughes

This poem acts as an antidote to the preceding two. Here is the poet's exuberant notion of a right and proper funeral. It recalls the New Orleans second line jazz funerals with their unstoppable celebration of life.

STAR SYSTEM

The stars in their magnificent array
Look down upon the Earth, their cynosure,
Or so it seems. They are too far away,
In fact, to see a thing; hence they look pure
To us. They lack the textures of our globe,
So only we, from cameras carried high,
Enjoy the beauty of the swirling robe
That wraps us up, the interplay of sky
And cloud, as if a Wedgwood plate of blue
And white should melt, and then, its surface stirred
With spoons, a treasure too good to be true,
Be placed, and hover like a hummingbird,
Drawing all eyes, though ours alone, to feast
On splendor as it turns west from the East.

There was a time when some of our young men
Walked plumply on the moon and saw Earth rise,
As stunning as the sun. The years since then
Have aged them. Now and then somebody dies.
It's like a clock, for those of us who saw
The Saturn rockets going up as if
Mankind had energy to burn. The law is
Is different for one man. Time is a cliff
You come to in the dark. Though you might fall
As easily as on a feather bed,
It is a sad farewell. You loved it all.
You dream that you might keep it in your head.
But memories, where can you take them to?
Take one last look at them. They end with you.

And still the Earth revolves, and still the blaze
Of stars maintains a show of vigilance.
It should, for long ago, in olden days,
We came from there. By luck, by fate, by chance,
All of the elements that form the world
Were sent by cataclysms deep in space,
And from their combination life unfurled
And stood up straight, and wore a human face.
I still can't pass a mirror. Like a boy,
I check my looks, and now I see the shell
Of what I was. So why, then, this strange joy?
Perhaps an old man dying would do well
To smile as he rejoins the cosmic dust
Life comes from, for resign himself he must.

Clive James

THE SNOW MAN

One must have a mind of winter
To regard the frost and the boughs
Of the pine-trees encrusted with snow;

And have been cold a long time
To behold the junipers shagged with ice,
The spruces rough in the distant glitter

Of the January sun; and not to think
Of any misery in the sound of the wind,
In the sound of a few leaves,

Which is the sound of the land
Full of the same wind
That is blowing in the same bare place

For the listener, who listens in the snow,
And, nothing himself, beholds
Nothing that is not there and the nothing that is.

Wallace Stevens

INTIMATIONS OF MORTALITY

Something that has no existence is absent here
and that absence is louder than any sound.
You have been hearing it all your life
and will hear it
till it grows so faint it overwhelms everything—
as a summer cloud
no bigger than your hand
will blot out the sunset that was never really there.

John Hall Wheelock

The title of this poem is a play on the title of William Wordsworth's famous poem "Intimations of Immortality." In that poem Wordsworth looks back on his childhood; here Wheelock looks forward toward his death. The poem keeps contradicting itself in its attempts to express the inexpressible: the ineffable nature of death.

OLD AGE

In me is a little painted square
Bordered by old shops with gaudy awnings.
And before the shops sit smoking, open-bloused old men,
Drinking sunlight.
The old men are my thoughts;
And I come to them each evening, in a creaking cart,
And quietly unload supplies.
We fill slim pipes and chat
And inhale scents from pale flowers in the center of the
      square....
Strong men, tinkling women, and dripping, squealing children
Stroll past us, or into the shops.
They greet the shopkeepers and touch their hats or
      foreheads to me....
Some evening I shall not return to my people.

Maxwell Bodenheim

This tender picture of old age and its peaceful ending belies the tragic later life and death of Bodenheim. The fact that he could write such a poem, when in reality for much of his life he was homeless and penniless, makes it all the more touching.

FOR THE ANNIVERSARY OF MY DEATH

Every year without knowing it I have passed the day
When the last fires will wave to me
And the silence will set out
Tireless traveler
Like the beam of a lightless star

Then I will no longer
Find myself in life as in a strange garment
Surprised at the earth
And the love of one woman
And the shamelessness of men
As today writing after three days of rain
Hearing the wren sing and the falling cease
And bowing not knowing to what

W. S. Merwin

THE COSSACKS

for F.

For Jews, the Cossacks are always coming.
Therefore I think the sun spot on my arm
is melanoma. Therefore I celebrate
New Year's Eve by counting
my annual dead.

My mother, when she was dying,
spoke to her visitors of books
and travel, displaying serenity
as a form of manners, though
I could tell the difference.

But when I watched you planning
for a life you knew
you'd never have, I couldn't explain
your genuine smile in the face
of disaster. Was it denial

laced with acceptance? Or was it
generations of being English —
Brontë's Lucy in *Villette*
living as if no fire raged
beneath her dun-colored dress.

I want to live the way you did,
preparing for next year's famine with wine
and music as if it were a ten-course banquet.
But listen: those are hoofbeats
on the frosty autumn air.

Linda Pastan

The Cossacks were Russian military groups who led the vicious anti-Jewish pogroms that took place during the nineteenth and twentieth centuries. In Pastan's poem they are equated with death.

A CONTRIBUTION TO STATISTICS

Out of a hundred people

those who always know better
—fifty-two

doubting every step
—nearly all the rest,

glad to lend a hand
if it doesn't take too long
—as high as forty-nine,

always good
because they can't be otherwise
—four, well maybe five,

able to admire without envy
—eighteen,

suffering illusions
induced by fleeting youth
—sixty, give or take a few,

not to be taken lightly
—forty and four,

living in constant fear
of someone or something
—seventy-seven,

capable of happiness
—twenty-something tops,

harmless singly, savage in crowds
—half at least,

cruel
when forced by circumstances
—better not to know
even ballpark figures,

wise after the fact
—just a couple more
than wise before it,

taking only things from life
—thirty
(I wish I were wrong),

hunched in pain,
no flashlight in the dark
—eighty-three
sooner or later,

righteous
—thirty-five, which is a lot,

righteous
and understanding
—three,

worthy of compassion
—ninety-nine

mortal
—a hundred out of a hundred.
Thus far this figure still remains unchanged.

Wislawa Szymborska
(translated from the Polish by
Stanislaw Baranczak and Clare Cavanagh)

Here statistics are a jumping-off platform for what appears at first to be a rather playful assessment of our lives but soon morphs into something else. Each stanza of the poem relies on actual statistics, compiled by the author herself in a survey of one hundred people.

IN THE BORDERLANDS

The part of this being that is rock,
the part of this body that is star,
lately I feel them yearning to go back
and be what they are.

As we get closer to the border
they whisper sometimes to my soul:
So long we've been away from order,
O when will we be whole?

Soon enough, my soul replies,
you'll shine in star and sleep in stone,
when I who troubled you a while with eyes
and grief and wakefulness am gone.

Ursula K. Le Guin

The idea that we are part of this universe before as well as after our individual incarnations is a definition of eternal life not encompassed by most Western theologies.

7

"YES, THAT WAS I"

Old age may surprise us. If it is not Robert Browning's romanticized "Grow old along with me! / The best is yet to be," neither is it merely the last station stop before oblivion. Like all that has gone before, it has its own distinct flavor, not to be known until actually tasted.

The edifice of old age is built on all that has come before, transformed into memories. These touchstones inform and enrich the present; indeed, they are what make us who we are. It is probably no accident that as we grow older we spend more time looking back on our pasts, trying to connect who we were with who we have become. We may once again take up some of the interests and pleasures of our youth. All of this seems to be a knitting together of past and present, a consolidation of all we have experienced.

In "Tradition and the Individual Talent," T. S. Eliot quoted someone who said to him, "The dead writers are remote from us because we know so much more than they did." And Eliot responded, "Precisely, and they are what we know." Likewise *we*—our former selves—are what *we* know. Our own pasts are the elements out of which we construct our present selves, who will continue to evolve into our future selves until the very end.

I BEGIN TO LOVE

I begin to love the beauty
of the old more than the beauty of
the young—the old lady shielding
her face from the hot sun with a black
lacy fan and the exquisite
old man with the white beard and the old man pushing
the cart of the young man dying
of dystrophy & the elderly
woman in black holding the hand of a little
child in an apricot smock.

Hilda Morley

THAT WAS I

I was that older man you saw sitting
in a confetti of yellow light and falling leaves
on a bench at the empty horseshoe courts
in Thayer, Nebraska — brown jacket, soft cap,
wiping my glasses. I had noticed, of course,
that the rows of sunken horseshoe pits
with their rusty stakes, grown over with grass,
were like old graves, but I was not letting
my thoughts go there. Instead I was looking
with hope to a grapevine draped over
a fence in a neighboring yard, and knowing
that I could hold on. Yes, that was I.

And that was I, the round-shouldered man
you saw that afternoon in Rising City
as you drove past the abandoned Mini Golf,
fists deep in my pockets, nose dripping,
as I walked the miniature Main Street
peering into the child-size plywood store,
the poor red school, the faded barn, thinking
that not even in such an abbreviated world
with no more than its little events — the snap
of a grasshopper's wing against a paper cup —
could a person control this life. Yes, that was I.

And that was I you spotted that evening
just before dark, in a weedy cemetery
west of Staplehurst, down on one knee
as if trying to make out the name on a stone,
some lonely old man, you thought, come there
to pity himself in a reliable sadness

of grass among graves, but that was not so.
Instead I had found in its perfect web
a handsome black and yellow spider
pumping its legs to try to shake my footing
as if I were a gift, an enormous moth
that it could snare and eat. Yes, that was I.

Ted Kooser

AFTER LONG SILENCE

Speech after long silence; it is right,
All other lovers being estranged or dead,
Unfriendly lamplight hid under its shade,
The curtains drawn upon unfriendly night,
That we descant and yet again descant
Upon the supreme theme of Art and Song:
Bodily decrepitude is wisdom; young
We loved each other and were ignorant.

W. B. Yeats

I DREAMED THAT I WAS OLD

I dreamed that I was old: in stale declension
Fallen from my prime, when company
Was mine, cat-nimbleness, and green invention,
Before time took my leafy hours away.

My wisdom, ripe with body's ruin, found
Itself tart recompense for what was lost
In false exchange: since wisdom in the ground
Has no apocalypse or pentecost.

I wept for my youth, sweet passionate young thought,
And cozy women dead that by my side
Once lay: I wept with bitter longing, not
Remembering how in my youth I cried.

Stanley Kunitz

Mourning one's lost youth is a familiar poetic trope. Late wisdom matters little; the cost of age weighs on the poet with no apparent compensatory gain. But then comes the final line.

"Apocalypse" and "pentecost" are biblical terms. "Apocalypse" means the complete and final destruction of the world, as described in the New Testament Book of Revelation. "Pentecost" is the Christian celebration of the descent of the Holy Spirit on the apostles.

CARPE DIEM

Age saw two quiet children
Go loving by at twilight,
He knew not whether homeward,
Or outward from the village,
Or (chimes were ringing) churchward.
He waited (they were strangers)
Till they were out of hearing
To bid them both be happy.
"Be happy, happy, happy,
And seize the day of pleasure."
The age-long theme is Age's.
'Twas Age imposed on poems
Their gather-roses burden
To warn against the danger
That overtaken lovers
From being overflooded
With happiness should have it
And yet not know they have it.
But bid life seize the present?
It lives less in the present
Than in the future always,
And less in both together

Than in the past. The present
Is too much for the senses,
Too crowding, too confusing—
Too present to imagine.

Robert Frost

Seize the day! We are constantly urged to live in the present moment. All well and good in theory, says Frost, but in reality impossible since the present overwhelms us. Virginia Woolf puts it this way: "The past is beautiful because one never realises an emotion at the time. It expands later, and thus we don't have complete emotions about the present, only about the past" (*The Diary of Virginia Woolf, Volume 3: 1925–1930*).

THEY

I see you down there, white-haired
among the green leaves,
picking the ripe raspberries,
and I think, "Forty-two years!"
We are the you and I who were
once the they whom we remember.

Wendell Berry

The grand mystery of time and aging is expressed succinctly in this small gem of a poem whose colors — white and green and red — flash before our eyes.

WHY SHOULD NOT OLD MEN BE MAD?

Why should not old men be mad?
Some have known a likely lad
That had a sound fly-fisher's wrist
Turn to a drunken journalist;
A girl that knew all Dante once
Live to bear children to a dunce;
A Helen of social welfare dream
Climb on a wagonette to scream.
Some think it a matter of course that chance
Should starve good men and bad advance,
That if their neighbours figured plain,
As though upon a lighted screen,
No single story would they find
Of an unbroken happy mind,
A finish worthy of the start.
Young men know nothing of this sort,
Observant old men know it well;
And when they know what old books tell,
And that no better can be had,
Know why an old man should be mad.

W. B. Yeats

FORGETFULNESS

The name of the author is the first to go
followed obediently by the title, the plot,
the heartbreaking conclusion, the entire novel
which suddenly becomes one you have never read, never even
    heard of,

as if, one by one, the memories you used to harbor
decided to retire to the southern hemisphere of the brain,
to a little fishing village where there are no phones.

Long ago you kissed the names of the nine Muses goodbye
and watched the quadratic equation pack its bag,
and even now as you memorize the order of the planets,

something else is slipping away, a state flower perhaps,
the address of an uncle, the capital of Paraguay.

Whatever it is you are struggling to remember,
it is not poised on the tip of your tongue,
not even lurking in some obscure corner of your spleen.

It has floated away down a dark mythological river
whose name begins with an L as far as you can recall

well on your own way to oblivion where you will join those
who have even forgotten how to swim and how to ride a bicycle.

No wonder you rise in the middle of the night
to look up the date of a famous battle in a book on war.
No wonder the moon in the window seems to have drifted
out of a love poem that you used to know by heart.

Billy Collins

In this description of the slow slippage of memory, there is some comfort in
knowing we have the delightful company of Collins on the slide.

THERE'S THE RUB

Envying young poets the rage
You wish you could reverse your night
And blaze out born on every page
As old as them, as debut-bright.

Child of that prodigal spotlight
Whose wattage now is theirs to wage—
What gold star rite you wish you might
Raise revised to its first prize stage.

But listen to my wizened sage:
He claims there's one disadvantage
Should time renew you neophyte—

There'd be one catch you'd hate, one spite:
Remember if you were their age
You'd have to write the way they write.

Bill Knott

Each generation creates its own vocabulary, its own currency. And each generation is in thrall to the language of its time.

YOUTH AND AGE

I remember when I was little and the world was great
A storm crashed the trees, lightnings vociferated,
Dark horror darkened the house, we descended
To the cellar in cold fear, in stupefying dread,
In wordless terror. I clung to the skirts of my mother.

Now I am old, and life continues, time is small.
Facing whatever may bring the end of the world
I have no better answer, now than then—
Blind clutches against the force of nature,
A wild glimpse, and poetry.

Richard Eberhart

Fearful of what the future may bring, both to himself and to the planet, the
poet turns to poetry as a bulwark against despair.

WITH AGE WISDOM

At twenty, stooping round about,
I thought the world a miserable place,
Truth a trick, faith in doubt,
Little beauty, less grace.

Now at sixty what I see,
Although the world is worse by far,
Stops my heart in ecstasy.
God, the wonders that there are!

Archibald MacLeish

After serving in World War I, MacLeish believed that the conflict marked the ending of an old order and the beginning of a new, a hope that resulted in disappointment. This small poem may act as a reminder of the change of perspective that age can bring, whatever the current state of the world.

8

"A SOLACE OF RIPE PLUMS"

By the time we have reached the proverbial three score and ten and counting, even the most fortunate among us have known stress and sorrow. At these times, assailed by events outside ourselves or demons within, we cast about for sources of consolation that can support and sustain us.

Among these sources is poetry. Poets who have found themselves in similar situations write in ways that connect to our own experience and may provide an expansion of our own understanding. It may be as simple as the taste of a ripe plum in William Carlos Williams's poem or as counterintuitive as the "banalities" of a poor island town as seen by Derek Walcott. To sit with a friend and read poems aloud to each other is a wonderful way to cope with a gray day.

Humor especially can lift us out of self-pity and depression; never discount the power of laughter, even in the hardest times. Thus we begin this section with two poems that, even as they deal with weighty matters, do so in a lighthearted style.

QUIET

Prolonged exposure to death
Has made my friend quieter.

Now his nose is less like a hatchet
And more like a snuffler.

Flames don't erupt from his mouth anymore
And life doesn't crack his thermometer.

Instead of overthrowing the government
He reads fly-fishing catalogues

And takes photographs of water.
An aphorist would say

The horns of the steer have grown straighter.
He has an older heart

That beats younger.
His Attila the Hun imitation

Is not as good as it used to be.
Everything else is better.

Tony Hoagland

A FINISHED MAN

Of the four louts who threw him off the dock
Three are now dead, and so more faintly mock
The way he choked and splashed and was afraid.
His memory of the fourth begins to fade.

It was himself whom he could not forgive;
Yet it has been a comfort to outlive
That woman, stunned by his appalling gaffe,
Who with a napkin half-suppressed her laugh,

Or that grey colleague, surely gone by now,
Who, turning toward the window, raised his brow,
Embarrassed to have caught him in a lie.
All witness darkens, eye by dimming eye.

Thus he can walk today with heart at ease
Through the old quad, escorted by trustees,
To dedicate the monumental gym
A grateful college means to name for him.

Seated, he feels the warm sun sculpt his cheek
As the young president gets up to speak.
If the dead die, if he can but forget,
If money talks, he may be perfect yet.

Richard Wilbur

PROVIDE, PROVIDE

The witch that came (the withered hag)
To wash the steps with pail and rag
Was once the beauty Abishag,

The picture pride of Hollywood.
Too many fall from great and good
For you to doubt the likelihood.

Die early and avoid the fate.
Or if predestined to die late,
Make up your mind to die in state.

Make the whole stock exchange your own!
If need be occupy a throne,
Where nobody can call *you* crone.

Some have relied on what they knew,
Others on simply being true.
What worked for them might work for you.

No memory of having starred
Atones for later disregard
Or keeps the end from being hard.

Better to go down dignified
With boughten friendship at your side
Than none at all. Provide, provide!

Robert Frost

Frost's wry New England voice comes through here in this satirical prescription for dealing with the inevitable losses of old age.

Abishag was the young beauty chosen to serve the biblical king and psalmist David in his old age. Among her duties was to lie next to him in bed in order to keep him warm.

COUNTRY STARS

The nearsighted child has taken off her glasses
and come downstairs to be kissed goodnight.
She blows on a black windowpane until it's white.
Over the apple trees a great bear passes
but she puts her own construction on the night.

Two cities, a chemical plant, and clotted cars
breathe our distrust of darkness on the air,
clouding the pane between us and the stars.
But have no fear, or only proper fear:
the bright watchers are still there.

William Meredith

This poem was published in 1976. Since then the world has undergone cata-
clysmic changes. What now is "proper fear"?

WHY WE MUST STRUGGLE

If we have not struggled
as hard as we can
at our strongest
how will we sense
the shape of our losses
or know what sustains
us longest or name
what change costs us,
saying how strange
it is that one sector
of the self can step in
for another in trouble,
how loss activates
a latent double, how
we can feed
as upon nectar
upon need?

Kay Ryan

ALLEGRO

After a black day, I play Haydn,
and feel a little warmth in my hands.

The keys are ready. Kind hammers fall.
The sound is spirited, green, and full of silence.

The sound says that freedom exists
and someone pays no tax to Caesar.

I shove my hands in my haydnpockets
and act like a man who is calm about it all.

I raise my haydnflag. The signal is:
"We do not surrender. But want peace."

The music is a house of glass standing on a slope;
rocks are flying, rocks are rolling.

The rocks roll straight through the house
but every pane of glass is still whole.

Tomas Tranströmer
(translated from the Swedish by Robert Bly)

Music can reach us in our deepest being, even in times of greatest despair.
Tranströmer suffered a paralytic stroke in 1990 and lost his power of speech,
but went on writing poetry until his death twenty-five years later.

TO A POOR OLD WOMAN

munching a plum on
the street a paper bag
of them in her hand

They taste good to her
They taste good
to her. They taste
good to her

You can see it by
the way she gives herself
to the one half
sucked out in her hand

Comforted
a solace of ripe plums
seeming to fill the air
They taste good to her

William Carlos Williams

CONSOLATION

How agreeable it is not to be touring Italy this summer,
wandering her cities and ascending her torrid hill towns.
How much better to cruise these local, familiar streets,
fully grasping the meaning of every road sign and billboard
and all the sudden hand gestures of my compatriots.

There are no abbeys here, no crumbling frescoes or famous
domes and there is no need to memorize a succession
of kings or tour the dripping corners of a dungeon.
No need to stand around a sarcophagus, see Napoleon's
little bed on Elba, or view the bones of a saint under glass.

How much better to command the simple precinct of home
than be dwarfed by pillar, arch, and basilica.
Why hide my head in phrase books and wrinkled maps?
Why feed scenery to a hungry, one-eyed camera
eager to eat the world one monument at a time?

Instead of slouching in a café ignorant of the word for ice,
I will head down to the coffee shop and the waitress
known as Dot. I will slide into the flow of the morning
paper, all language barriers down,
rivers of idiom running freely, eggs over easy on the way.

And after breakfast, I will not have to find someone
willing to photograph me with my arm around the owner.
I will not puzzle over the bill or record in a journal
what I had to eat and how the sun came in the window.
It is enough to climb back into the car

as if it were the great car of English itself
and sounding my loud vernacular horn, speed off
down a road that will never lead to Rome, not even Bologna.

Billy Collins

UNTITLED #51

No opera, no gilded columns, no wine-dark seas,
no Penelope scouring the stalls with delicate glasses,
no practiced ecstasy from the tireless tenor, no sweets
and wine at no interval, no altos, no basses
and violins sobbing as one; no opera house,
no museum, no actual theatre, no civic center
—and what else? Only the huge doors of clouds
with the setting disc through which we leave and enter,
only the deafening parks with their jumping crowds,
and the thudding speakers. Only the Government
Buildings down by the wharf, and another cruise ship
big as the capital, all blue glass and cement.
No masterpieces in huge frames to worship.
On such banalities has life been spent
in brightness, and yet there are the days
when every street corner rounds itself into
a sunlit surprise, a painting or a phrase,
canoes drawn up by the market, the harbour's blue,
the barracks. So much to do still, all of it praise.

Derek Walcott

Like the preceding poem, this one opens with a series of negatives. They are contrasted with the "banalities," the homely familiar sights and places in Saint Lucia, the Caribbean island where Walcott was born and trained as a painter. The poem's conclusion is the result of a lifetime of travel and experience. If Walcott had never left the island, would he have felt the same way?

Penelope was the wife of Odysseus who remained faithful to him during his long absence.

OUT OF A DARK WOOD

Out of a dark wood we stumble, spirit-led,
Out of a grief find comfort in a grace of grief,
Sorrow that rounds the shape of blessings
As the painter's brush, shadow or high-light, touched,
Rounds out the shape of fruit, the light of an eye,
Defines the nervous finger of a quiet hand,
sorrow, the shadow of our joy, bright memories,
Lifted and bound as in a child's bouquet,
sorrow to leave all that we bless to-day,
To-day, mortal in time, in quality
formed not to stay —
So sorrow, bless us before we go away.

Janet Lewis

Lewis, who lived until almost a hundred, wrote this beautifully crafted poem in her nineties. Elegiac in tone, this is an ode to sorrow and how it mysteriously underlies and defines our pleasures.

9

"LATE RIPENESS"

This section begins with a poem by D. H. Lawrence in which a young man imagines what an ideal old age should be. Since Lawrence died at forty-four, he never got there himself; but we can be fairly certain that it would not have been as he had envisioned.

And would we, who are actually old, want it to be as he imagines? His romanticized, even clichéd, view of age as a ripened apple omits the tartness, the bite, the pith of the actual fruit. New experiences don't stop with a certain birthday, nor are surprises limited to the young. And if losses are inevitable, the pleasures that remain may be intensified or replaced by others equally satisfying.

BEAUTIFUL OLD AGE

It ought to be lovely to be old
to be full of the peace that comes of experience
and wrinkled ripe fulfilment.

The wrinkled smile of completeness that follows a life
lived undaunted and unsoured with accepted lies
if people lived without accepting lies
they would ripen like apples, and be scented like pippins
in their old age.

Soothing, old people should be, like apples
when one is tired of love.
Fragrant like yellowing leaves, and dim with the soft
stillness and satisfaction of autumn.

And a girl should say:
It must be wonderful to live and grow old.
Look at my mother, how rich and still she is!—

And a young man should think: By Jove
my father has faced all weathers, but it's been a life!

D. H. Lawrence

This poem is replete with prescriptive "shoulds." We are told what old age ought to be. How close does it come to our own experience and/or desires?

GETTING OLDER

The first surprise: I like it.
Whatever happens now, some things
that used to terrify have not:

I didn't die young, for instance. Or lose
my only love. My three children
never had to run away from anyone.

Don't tell me this gratitude is complacent.
We all approach the edge of the same blackness
which for me is silent.

Knowing as much sharpens
my delight in January freesia,
hot coffee, winter sunlight. So we say

as we lie close on some gentle occasion:
every day won from such
darkness is a celebration.

Elaine Feinstein

As we reach old age, we each begin to accumulate our own unique store of days "won from…darkness."

HAND-ME-DOWNS

My love rests on the couch
in the sweater and bones of old age

I have stopped reading to look at him   I take
his hand   I am shawled in my own somewhat
wrinkled still serviceable skin

No one knows what to do with these
hand-me-downs   love them I suppose

weren't they worn in and out of
dignity by our mothers and
fathers   even our children in
the grip of merciless genes will
wear these garments

may their old lovers greet and
touch them then in the bare light
of that last beauty

Grace Paley

OLD IS FOR BOOKS

A poet named Robert Browning eloped with a poetess
  named Elizabeth Barrett,
And since he had an independent income they lived in an
  Italian villa instead of a London garret.
He created quite a furor
With his elusive caesura.
He also created a youthful sage,
A certain Rabbi Ben Ezra, who urged people to hurry up
  and age.
This fledgling said, "Grow old along with me!
The best is yet to be..."
I term him fledgling because such a statement, certes,
Could emanate only from a youngster in his thirties.
I have a friend named Ben Azzara, who is far from a fledgling;
Indeed, he is more like from the bottom of the sea of life a
  barnacled dredgling.
He tells me that as the years have slipped by
He has become utterly dependent on his wife because he
  has forgotten how to tie his tie.
He says he sleeps after luncheon instead of at night,
And he hates to face his shaving mirror because although
  his remaining hair is brown his mustache comes out red
  and his beard comes out white.
Furthermore, he says that last week he was stranded for
  thirty-six hours in his club
Because he couldn't get out of the tub.

He says he was miserable, but when he reflected that the
    same thing probably eventually happened to Rabbi
    Ben Ezra
It relieved his mizra.

Ogden Nash

Nash seems unconvinced by the previous poem's lofty sentiments.

RABBI BEN EZRA (*EXCERPT*)

Grow old along with me!
  The best is yet to be,
The last of life, for which the first was made:
  Our times are in His hand
  Who saith "A whole I planned,
Youth shows but half; trust God: see all nor be afraid!"

                                    Robert Browning

Rabbi Abraham ben Meir ibn Ezra was a medieval Jewish biblical scholar born in Spain. This excerpt is the most well-known part of a much longer poem, a meditation on his life and work.

UNTITLED

Though not occasioned
to mirror watching
    I stopped
and saw delightedly
    star streaks, grey lights
moving through my hair.
I was mother-reflection
then, my mother watching me
becoming old as she had not
lived to do.
    I cannot know
what she would have felt
as age came on in silence,
but I dance elated on seeing
touches of silver
    appearing unasked
but earned by living
as widely as I dare.

Kathian Poulton

GLASS

I'd have thought by now it would have stopped,
as anything sooner or later will stop, but still it happens

that when I unexpectedly catch sight of myself in a mirror,
there's a kind of concussion, a cringe; I look quickly away.

Lately, since my father died and I've come close to his age,
I sometimes see him first, and have to focus to find myself.

I've thought it's that, my precious singularity being diluted,
but it's harsher than that, crueler, the way, when I was young,

I believed how you looked was supposed to *mean,*
something graver, more substantial: I'd gaze at my poor face

and think, "It's still not there." Apparently I still do.
What isn't there? Beauty? Not likely. Wisdom? Less.

Is how we live or try to live supposed to embellish us?
All I see is the residue of my other, failed faces.

But maybe what we're after is just a less abrasive regard:
not "It's still not there," but something like "Come in, be still."

C. K. Williams

YOUTHFUL ELD

Young men dancing, and the old
Sporting I with joy behold;
But an old man gay and free
Dancing most I love to see;
Age and youth alike he shares,
For his heart belies his hairs.

Anacreon
(translated from the Greek by Thomas Stanley)

LATE RIPENESS

Not soon, as late as the approach of my ninetieth year,
I felt a door opening in me and I entered
the clarity of early morning.

One after another my former lives were departing,
like ships, together with their sorrow.

And the countries, cities, gardens, the bays of seas
assigned to my brush came closer,
ready now to be described better than they were before.

I was not separated from my people,
grief and pity joined us.
We forget—I kept saying—that we are all children of the King.

For where we come from there is no division
into Yes and No, into is, was, and will be.

We were miserable, we used no more than a hundredth part
of the gift we received for our long journey.

Moments from yesterday and from centuries ago—
a sword blow, the painting of eyelashes before a mirror
of polished metal, a lethal musket shot, a caravel
staving its hull against a reef—they dwell in us,
waiting for a fulfillment.

I knew, always, that I would be a worker in the vineyard,
as are all men and women living at the same time,
whether they are aware of it or not.

Czeslaw Milosz
(translated from the Polish by
Robert Hass and Czeslaw Milosz)

As of this writing, there are approximately 7,730,000,000 people alive in the world, all of them our contemporaries, experiencing the very same time under the sun and stars. This is the vision of "no division" that Milosz achieved in his old age and wished for all humankind.

RECONSIDERATION

I thought I'd give my face a gift—
A nip, a tuck, a little lift,
But then I thought how long it took
To give my face its weathered look,
The years it took to crease this brow;
And so I put it off for now.
I once was young. That tale's been told.
But only lucky folk grow old.

Mary Ann Hoberman

A FACE, A CUP

The thousand hairline cracks in an aged face
match the hairline cracks in an aged cup
and come from similar insults: careless, base
self-absorbed gestures from a younger face,
cruel and fine. Bang! Each disturbed trace
deepens to a visible crack. A break-up,
a mix-up, a wild mistake: these show in a face
like the hairline cracks in an ancient cup.

Neither wholly broken nor all used up
the cup becomes a visage, unstable.
One never knows what will crack it open
and finish it. Banged too hard on a table?
Yet happiness might crack a face open
in a better way: as laugh lines
releasing the joys of ancient thoughts
cupped into use, and suddenly able.

Molly Peacock

Carrying this comparison throughout the poem, the poet arrives at an alternate interpretation of those "hairline cracks," now evidence of old joys.

TERMINUS

It is time to be old,
To take in sail:—
The god of bounds,
Who sets to seas a shore,
Came to me in his fatal rounds,
And said: "No more!
No farther shoot
Thy broad ambitious branches, and thy root.
Fancy departs: no more invent;
Contract thy firmament
To compass of a tent.
There's not enough for this and that,
Make thy option which of two;
Economize the failing river,
Not the less revere the Giver,
Leave the many and hold the few.
Timely wise accept the terms,
Soften the fall with wary foot;
A little while
Still plan and smile,
And,—fault of novel germs,—
Mature the unfallen fruit.
Curse, if thou wilt, thy sires,
Bad husbands of their fires,
Who, when they gave thee breath,
Failed to bequeath
The needful sinew stark as once,
The Baresark marrow to thy bones,
But left a legacy of ebbing veins,
Inconstant heat and nerveless reins,—
Amid the Muses, left thee deaf and dumb,
Amid the gladiators, halt and numb."

As the bird trims her to the gale,
I trim myself to the storm of time,
I man the rudder, reef the sail,
Obey the voice at eve obeyed at prime:
"Lowly faithful, banish fear,
Right onward drive unharmed;
The port, well worth the cruise, is near,
And every wave is charmed."

Ralph Waldo Emerson

"You cannot control the winds but you can adjust the sails." Here Emerson seems to flesh out this familiar adage by Anonymous, transforming it into a positive prescription for living that has sustained readers since its publication in 1867. A "baresark" is a berserker or Norse warrior who fought without armor.

MOTHER TO SON

Well, son, I'll tell you:
Life for me ain't been no crystal stair.
It's had tacks in it,
And splinters,
And boards torn up,
And places with no carpet on the floor—
Bare.
But all the time
I'se been a-climbin' on,
And reachin' landin's,
And turnin' corners,
And sometimes goin' in the dark
Where there ain't been no light.
So boy, don't you turn back.
Don't you set down on the steps
'Cause you finds it's kinder hard.
Don't you fall now—
For I'se still goin', honey,
I'se still climbin',
And life for me ain't been no crystal stair.

Langston Hughes

10

"GLAD TO THE BRINK OF FEAR"

Ralph Waldo Emerson's description of joy, quoted by Denise Levertov in her poem "Joy," is on the face of it an oxymoron. How can joy and fear be related? There is something in the fleeting nature of joy, in its unexpectedness and evanescence, that makes it especially precious. It comes and goes without our bidding. Clutch at it and it will vanish. Therein lies the fear.

This sense of joy can occur at any age. Suddenly, often for no discernible reason, we are bathed in a feeling of inextricable well-being. We are at one with creation; all's right with the world.

Memories of these moments of grace stay with us throughout our lives. Weightless in themselves, they nevertheless provide a counterweight to the everyday. However, the real magic occurs when it is everyday life itself that occasions this joyfulness.

WHY

Why all the embarrassment
about being happy?
Sometimes I'm as happy
as a sleeping dog,
and for the same reasons,
and for others.

Wendell Berry

WORDS FROM THE FRONT

We don't look as young
as we used to
except in dim light
especially in
the soft warmth of candlelight
when we say
in all sincerity
You're so cute
and
You're my cutie.
Imagine
two old people
behaving like this.
It's enough
to make you happy.

Ron Padgett

ONE OF THE BUTTERFLIES

The trouble with pleasure is the timing
it can overtake me without warning
and be gone before I know it is here
it can stand facing me unrecognized
while I am remembering somewhere else
in another age or someone not seen
for years and never to be seen again
in this world and it seems I cherish
only now a joy I was not aware of
when it was here although it remains
out of reach and will not be caught or named
or called back and if I could make it stay
as I want to it would turn into pain

W. S. Merwin

JOY

> You must love the crust of the earth
> on which you dwell. You must be
> able to extract nutriment out of a
> sandheap. You must have so good
> an appetite as this, else you will
> live in vain.
>
> *Thoreau*

Joy, the, "well...*joyfulness* of
joy"—"many years
I had known it," the woman of eighty
said, "only remembered, till now."

Traherne
in dark fields.
          On Tremont Street,
on the Common, a raw dusk, Emerson
"glad to the brink of fear."
          It is objective,

stands founded, a roofed gateway;
we cloud-wander

away from it, stumble
again towards it not seeing it,

enter cast-down, discover ourselves
"in joy" as "in love."

Denise Levertov

A state of joy can be as vibrant as one of love and occur just as unexpectedly.

Thomas Traherne was a seventeenth-century English poet whose writings were suffused with spirituality.

"Crossing a bare common, in snow puddles, at twilight, under a clouded sky, without having in my thoughts any occurrence of special good fortune, I have enjoyed a perfect exhilaration. I am glad to the brink of fear." From Emerson's essay "Nature."

SONNET

Caught—the bubble
in the spirit-level,
a creature divided;
and the compass needle
wobbling and wavering,
undecided.
Freed—the broken
thermometer's mercury
running away;
and the rainbow-bird
from the narrow bevel
of the empty mirror,
flying wherever
it feels like, gay!

Elizabeth Bishop

This is the last, or nearly last, poem Bishop wrote, shortly before her death. Here she amuses herself by cutting her word count drastically, allowing her poem to "run away" free, like the liberated mercury, and fly like a bird to wherever it wishes.

ANY MORNING

Just lying on the couch and being happy.
Only humming a little, the quiet sound in the head.
Trouble is busy elsewhere at the moment, it has
so much to do in the world.

People who might judge are mostly asleep; they can't
monitor you all the time, and sometimes they forget.
When dawn flows over the hedge you can
get up and act busy.

Little corners like this, pieces of Heaven
left lying around, can be picked up and saved.
People won't even see that you have them,
they are so light and easy to hide.

Later in the day you can act like the others.
You can shake your head. You can frown.

William Stafford

GOOD

I bet
you'll see me in the park
strolling with a cane,
a bit wobbly now and then
which is good, for
why should ground be taken
for granted or trees?

I like
to lean my back against
a tamarack — straight in its majesty.
I swear I hear it hum
which is very good for
me since I need melodies
to remind me to hold up

and lean
into whatever is close
and near and could be dear
which is exceedingly good
to my mind, and could be
to yours. I know advice is
useless, but an example is
another thing.

I sit on a bench,
eat a sandwich, a bit mushed
in the pocket but tasty still
which is good since the truth is
that savoring is a necessity.
So I eat and tap my old feet

against
the pavement
and breathe which is good
for just about everything.
Then home like a horse
to its stable, recognizing
my small place in the world

there to be
with familiar things and sense
where I've landed for now, which is
better than good since it is
neither good nor bad—
but a joy if you know what I mean.
No comparison.

Gunilla Norris

FROM BLOSSOMS

From blossoms comes
this brown paper bag of peaches
we bought from the boy
at the bend in the road where we turned toward
signs painted *Peaches*.

From laden boughs, from hands,
from sweet fellowship in the bins,
comes nectar at the roadside, succulent
peaches we devour, dusty skin and all,
comes this familiar dust of summer, dust we eat.

O, to take what we love inside,
to carry within us an orchard, to eat
not only the skin, but the shade,
not only the sugar, but the days, to hold
the fruit in our hands, adore it, then bite into
the round jubilance of peach.

There are days we live
as if death were nowhere
in the background; from joy
to joy to joy, from wing to wing,
from blossom to blossom to
impossible blossom, to sweet impossible blossom.

Li-Young Lee

To savor fully the "round jubilance of peach" — with all that has made it what it is — is to savor creation.

WHAT ARE YEARS?

What is our innocence,
what is our guilt? All are
    naked, none is safe. And whence
is courage: the unanswered question,
the resolute doubt,—
dumbly calling, deafly listening—that
in misfortune, even death,
        encourages others
        and in its defeat, stirs

    the soul to be strong? He
sees deep and is glad, who
    accedes to mortality
and in his imprisonment rises
upon himself as
the sea in a chasm, struggling to be
free and unable to be,
        in its surrendering
        finds its continuing.

    So he who strongly feels,
behaves. The very bird,
    grown taller as he sings, steels
his form straight up. Though he is captive,
his mighty singing
says, satisfaction is a lowly
thing, how pure a thing is joy.
        This is mortality,
        This is eternity.

Marianne Moore

TODAY

If ever there were a spring day so perfect,
so uplifted by a warm intermittent breeze

that it made you want to throw
open all the windows in the house

and unlatch the door to the canary's cage
indeed, rip the little door from its jamb,

a day when the cool brick paths
and the garden bursting with peonies

seemed so etched in sunlight
that you felt like taking

a hammer to the glass paperweight
on the living room end table,

releasing the inhabitants
from their snow-covered cottage

so they could walk out,
holding hands and squinting

into this larger dome of blue and white,
well, today is just that kind of day.

Billy Collins

THE BLESSING OF THE OLD WOMAN, THE TULIP, AND THE DOG

To be blessed
said the old woman
is to live and work
so hard
God's love
washes right through you
like milk through a cow

To be blessed
said the dark red tulip
is to knock their eyes out
with the slug of lust
implied by
your up-ended skirt

To be blessed
said the dog
is to have a pinch
of God
inside you
and all the other
dogs can smell it

Alicia Ostriker

11

"TOWARD WHAT UNDREAMT CONDITION"

Despite all our puzzling and pondering, the mystery of life remains. But isn't this very quality of strangeness and impenetrability what gives life so much of its interest and savor? No matter how much we learn, there is always more to discover; no matter how far we have come, there is always farther to go.

We are each a small part of the great chain of being, and we leave this world to make way for the next links in the chain. Looked at in this way, death becomes a natural part of life, the final stage of our life here on earth but possibly the first stage of something as yet unknown. Who is to say? Each of us is free to make up our own mind.

From the very beginning of literature, poets have offered their individual views on this supreme mystery. Some of them follow.

THIS WORLD IS NOT CONCLUSION

This World is not Conclusion.
A Species stands beyond—
Invisible, as Music—
But positive, as Sound—
It beckons, and it baffles—
Philosophy—don't know—
And through a Riddle, at the last—
Sagacity, must go—
To guess it, puzzles scholars—
To gain it, Men have borne
Contempt of Generations
And Crucifixion, shown—
Faith slips—and laughs, and rallies—
Blushes, if any see—
Plucks at a twig of Evidence—
And asks a Vane, the way—
Much Gesture, from the Pulpit—
Strong Hallelujahs roll—
Narcotics cannot still the Tooth
That nibbles at the soul—

Emily Dickinson

Here Dickinson grapples once again with the ultimate mystery of existence. While she continued to question conventional religious belief throughout her life, she never relinquished her spiritual search.

WEAN YOURSELF

Little by little, wean yourself.

This is the gist of what I have to say.

From an embryo, whose nourishment comes in the blood,
move to an infant drinking milk,
to a child on solid food,
to a searcher after wisdom,
to a hunter of more invisible game.

Think how it is to have a conversation with an embryo.
You might say, "The world outside is vast and intricate.
There are wheatfields and mountain passes, and orchards
    in bloom.

At night there are millions of galaxies, and in sunlight
the beauty of friends dancing at a wedding."

You ask the embryo why he, or she, stays cooped up
in the dark with eyes closed.

                    Listen to the answer.

There is no "other world."
I only know what I've experienced.
You must be hallucinating.

                              Mathnawi, III, 49–6
                              Jalal al-Din Rumi
                    (translated from the Persian by Coleman Barks)

FINAL NOTATIONS

it will not be simple, it will not be long
it will take little time, it will take all your thought
it will take all your heart, it will take all your breath
it will be short, it will not be simple

it will touch through your ribs, it will take all your heart
it will not be long, it will occupy all your thought
as a city is occupied, as a bed is occupied
it will take all your flesh, it will not be simple

You are coming into us who cannot withstand you
you are coming into us who never wanted to withstand you
you are taking parts of us into places never planned
you are going far away with pieces of our lives

it will be short, it will take all your breath
it will not be simple, it will become your will

Adrienne Rich

THE WINDOW

A storm blew in last night and knocked out
the electricity. When I looked
through the window, the trees were translucent.
Bent and covered with rime. A vast calm
lay over the countryside.
I knew better. But at that moment
I felt I'd never in my life made any
false promises, not committed
so much as one indecent act. My thoughts
were virtuous. Later on that morning,
of course, electricity was restored.
The sun moved from behind the clouds,
melting the hoarfrost.
And things stood as they had before.

Raymond Carver

THE NIGHT MIGRATIONS

This is the moment when you see again
the red berries of the mountain ash
and in the dark sky
the birds' night migrations.

It grieves me to think
the dead won't see them —
these things we depend on,
they disappear.

What will the soul do for solace then?
I tell myself maybe it won't need
these pleasures anymore;
maybe just not being is simply enough,
hard as that is to imagine.

Louise Glück

SAILING TO BYZANTIUM

That is no country for old men. The young
In one another's arms, birds in the trees,
—Those dying generations—at their song,
The salmon-falls, the mackerel-crowded seas,
Fish, flesh, or fowl, commend all summer long
Whatever is begotten, born, and dies.
Caught in that sensual music all neglect
Monuments of unageing intellect.

An aged man is but a paltry thing,
A tattered coat upon a stick, unless
Soul clap its hands and sing, and louder sing
For every tatter in its mortal dress,
Nor is there singing school but studying
Monuments of its own magnificence;
And therefore I have sailed the seas and come
To the holy city of Byzantium.

O sages standing in God's holy fire
As in the gold mosaic of a wall,
Come from the holy fire, perne in a gyre,
And be the singing-masters of my soul.
Consume my heart away; sick with desire
And fastened to a dying animal
It knows not what it is; and gather me
Into the artifice of eternity.

Once out of nature I shall never take
My bodily form from any natural thing,
But such a form as Grecian goldsmiths make
Of hammered gold and gold enamelling

To keep a drowsy Emperor awake;
Or set upon a golden bough to sing
To lords and ladies of Byzantium
Of what is past, or passing, or to come.

                                                    W. B. Yeats

Once again, Yeats bemoans old age, but out of his despair he fashions one of his most glorious poems.

Byzantium, an ancient city of Thrace, was renamed Constantinople after the Roman emperor Constantine I. It is the site of the modern city of Istanbul, Turkey. During Constantine's reign, it was the capital of the Roman Empire and known for its great power and wealth. In a BBC radio broadcast in 1931 Yeats explained his choice of Byzantium as the central symbol of this poem: "I am trying to write about the state of my soul.…Byzantium was the centre of European civilization and the source of its spiritual philosophy, so I symbolize the search for the spiritual life by a journey to that city."

A MEASURING WORM

This yellow striped green
Caterpillar, climbing up
The steep window screen,

Constantly (for lack
Of a full set of legs) keeps
Humping up his back.

It's as if he sent
By a sort of semaphore
Dark omegas meant

To warn of Last Things.
Although he doesn't know it,
He will soon have wings,

And I, too, don't know
Toward what undreamt condition
Inch by inch I go.

Richard Wilbur

The measuring worm is the larval or caterpillar state of the geometer moth. Also called an inchworm because of its looping gait, it looks as if it is measuring the surface as it moves. When it is curled up, it resembles the last letter of the Greek alphabet, omega.

VESPERS

In your extended absence, you permit me
use of earth, anticipating
some return on investment. I must report
failure in my assignment, principally
regarding the tomato plants.
I think I should not be encouraged to grow
tomatoes. Or, if I am, you should withhold
the heavy rains, the cold nights that come
so often here, while other regions get
twelve weeks of summer. All this
belongs to you: on the other hand,
I planted the seeds, I watched the first shoots
like wings tearing the soil, and it was my heart
broken by the blight, the black spot so quickly
multiplying in the rows. I doubt
you have a heart, in our understanding of
that term. You who do not discriminate
between the dead and the living, who are, in consequence,
immune to foreshadowing, you may not know
how much terror we bear, the spotted leaf,
the red leaves of the maple falling
even in August, in early darkness: I am responsible
for these vines.

Louise Glück

"Vespers": a service of evening prayer.

NOTE: THE SEA GRINDS THINGS UP

It's going on now
as these words appear
to you or are heard by you.
A wave slaps down, flat.
Water runs up the beach,
then wheels and slides
back down, leaving a ridge
of sea-foam, weed, and shells.
One thinks: I must
break out of this
horrible cycle, but
the ocean doesn't: it
continues through the thought.
A wave breaks, some
of its water runs up
the beach and down
again, leaving a ridge
of scum and skeletal debris.
One thinks: I must
break out of this
cycle of life and death,
but the ocean doesn't: it
goes past the thought.
A wave breaks on the sand,
water planes up the beach
and wheels back down,
hissing and leaving a ridge
of anything it can leave.
One thinks: I must
run out the life

part of this cycle,
then the death part
of this cycle, and then
go on as the sea
goes on in this cycle
after the last word,
but this is not the last
word unless you think
of this cycle as some
perpetual inventory
of the sea. Remember:
this is just one sea
on one beach on one
planet in one
solar system in one
galaxy. After that
the scale increases, so
this is not the last word,
and nothing else is talking back.
It's a lonely situation.

Alan Dugan

THE WAY

The sky is random. Even calling it "sky"
is an attempt to make a meaning, say,
a shape, from the humanly visible part
of shapelessness in endlessness. It's what
we do, in some ways it's entirely what
we do — and so the devastating rose

of a galaxy's being born, the fatal lamé
of another's being torn and dying, we frame
in the lenses of our super-duper telescopes the way
we would those other completely incomprehensible
fecund and dying subjects at a family picnic.
Making them "subjects." "Rose." "Lamé." The way

our language scissors the enormity to scales
we can tolerate. The way we gild and rubricate
in memory, or edit out selectively.
An infant's gentle snoring, even, apportions
the eternal. When they moved to the boonies,
Dorothy Wordsworth measured their walk

to Crewkerne — then the nearest town —
by pushing a device invented especially
for such a project, a "perambulator": seven miles.
Her brother William pottered at his daffodils poem.
Ten thousand saw I at a glance: by which he meant
too many to count, but could only say it in counting.

                                        Albert Goldbarth

THE CITY LIMITS

When you consider the radiance, that it does not withhold
itself but pours its abundance without selection into every
nook and cranny not overhung or hidden; when you consider

that birds' bones make no awful noise against the light but
lie low in the light as in a high testimony; when you consider
the radiance, that it will look into the guiltiest

swervings of the weaving heart and bear itself upon them,
not flinching into disguise or darkening; when you consider
the abundance of such resource as illuminates the glow-blue

bodies and gold-skeined wings of flies swarming the dumped
guts of a natural slaughter or the coil of shit and in no
way winces from its storms of generosity; when you consider

that air or vacuum, snow or shale, squid or wolf, rose or lichen,
each is accepted into as much light as it will take, then
the heart moves roomier, the man stands and looks about, the

leaf does not increase itself above the grass, and the dark
work of the deepest cells is of a tune with May bushes
and fear lit by the breadth of such calmly turns to praise.

A. R. Ammons

12

"NOW FOR LUNCH"

So what have we learned from our journey through the words of the hundred or so poets whom we have met in the preceding pages? We, Carolyn and Mary Ann, the compilers of this anthology, hope that you, our readers, have been persuaded that poetry can make a real difference in your lives as it has in ours, that it can offer an oasis of peace and quiet amidst the clamor of modern existence. We hope, too, that you have discovered that poetry can provide increased access to your own inner world, that it can enrich your own thoughts, and that it can contribute new ideas and insights.

But above all, we wish that you may return to your own life with renewed hope and vigor, appreciating your own daily round and rejoicing in the marvel of the quotidian.

LEAST ACTION

Is it vision
or the lack
that brings me
back to the principle
of least action,
by which in one
branch of rabbinical
thought the world
might become the
Kingdom of Peace not
through the tumult
and destruction necessary
for a New Start but
by adjusting little parts
a little bit—turning
a cup a quarter inch
or scooting up a bench.
It imagines an
incremental resurrection,
a radiant body
puzzled out through
tinkering with the fit
of what's available.
As though what is is
right already but
askew. It is tempting
for any person who would
like to love what she
can do.

Kay Ryan

LOVE AFTER LOVE

The time will come
when, with elation
you will greet yourself arriving
at your own door, in your own mirror,
and each will smile at the other's welcome,

and say sit here. Eat.
You will love again the stranger who was your self.
Give wine. Give bread. Give back your heart
to itself, to the stranger who has loved you

all your life, whom you ignored
for another, who knows you by heart.
Take down the love-letters from the bookshelf,

the photographs, the desperate notes,
peel your own image from the mirror.
Sit. Feast on your life.

Derek Walcott

A LIVING

A man should never earn his living,
if he earns his life he'll be lovely.

A bird
picks up its seeds or little snails
between heedless earth and heaven
in heedlessness.

But, the plucky little sport, it gives to life
song, and chirruping, gay feathers, fluff-shadowed warmth
and all the unspeakable charm of birds hopping and fluttering
    and being birds,
— And we, we get it all from them for nothing.

D. H. Lawrence

THE WELL DRESSED MAN WITH A BEARD

After the final no there comes a yes
And on that yes the future world depends.
No was the night. Yes is the present sun.
If the rejected things, the things denied,
Slid over the western cataract, yet one,
One only, one thing that was firm, even
No greater than a cricket's horn, no more
Than a thought to be rehearsed all day, a speech
Of the self that must sustain itself on speech,
One thing remaining, infallible, would be
Enough. Ah! douce campagna of that thing!
Ah! douce campagna, honey in the heart,
Green in the body, out of a petty phrase,
Out of a thing believed, a thing affirmed:
The form on the pillow humming while one sleeps,
The aureole above the humming house . . .

It can never be satisfied, the mind, never.

Wallace Stevens

"Douce campagna," a conflation of French and Italian, means "pleasant plain"
or "sweet place."

AFTER READING A CHILD'S GUIDE TO
MODERN PHYSICS

If all a top physicist knows
About the Truth be true,
Then, for all the so-and-so's,
Futility and grime,
Our common world contains,
We have a better time
Than the Greater Nebulae do,
Or the atoms in our brains.

Marriage is rarely bliss
But, surely, it would be worse
As particles to pelt
At thousands of miles per sec
About a universe
In which a lover's kiss
Would either not be felt
Or break the loved one's neck.

Though the face at which I stare
While shaving it be cruel
For, year after year, it repels
An ageing suitor, it has,
Thank God, sufficient mass
To be altogether there,
Not an indeterminate gruel
Which is partly somewhere else.

Our eyes prefer to suppose
That a habitable place
Has a geocentric view,
That architects enclose

A quiet Euclidean space:
Exploded myths,—but who
Would feel at home astraddle
An ever expanding saddle?

This passion of our kind
For the process of finding out
Is a fact one can hardly doubt,
But I would rejoice in it more
If I knew more clearly what
We wanted the knowledge for,
Felt certain still that the mind
Is free to know or not.

It has chosen once, it seems,
And whether our concern
For magnitude's extremes
Really become a creature
Who comes in a median size,
Or politicising Nature
Be altogether wise,
Is something we shall learn.

W. H. Auden

Do we already know too much for our own good? And will further knowl-
edge contribute to our well-being? Stay tuned.

THE END AND THE BEGINNING

After every war
someone has to clean up.
Things won't
straighten themselves up, after all.

Someone has to push the rubble
to the side of the road,
so the corpse-filled wagons
can pass.

Someone has to get mired
in scum and ashes,
sofa springs,
splintered glass,
and bloody rags.

Someone has to drag in a girder
to prop up a wall.
Someone has to glaze a window,
rehang a door.

Photogenic it's not,
and takes years.
All the cameras have left
for another war.

We'll need the bridges back,
and new railway stations.
Sleeves will go ragged
from rolling them up.

Someone, broom in hand,
still recalls the way it was.

Someone else listens
and nods with unsevered head.
But already there are those nearby
starting to mill about
who will find it dull.

From out of the bushes
sometimes someone still unearths
rusted-out arguments
and carries them to the garbage pile.

Those who knew
what was going on here
must make way for
those who know little.
And less than little.
And finally as little as nothing.

In the grass that has overgrown
causes and effects,
someone must be stretched out,
blade of grass in his mouth
gazing at the clouds.

Wislawa Szymborska
(translated from the Polish by Joanna Trzeciak)

LOVE IS A PLACE

love is a place
& through this place of
love move
(with brightness of peace)
all places

yes is a word
& in this world of
yes live
(skillfully curled)
all worlds

E. E. Cummings

THE LEAKY FAUCET

All through the night, the leaky faucet
searches the stillness of the house
with its radar blip: who is awake?
Who lies out there as full of worry
as a pan in the sink? *Cheer up,*
cheer up, the little faucet calls,
someone will help you through your life.

Ted Kooser

TICKET

This is the ticket
I failed to spend.
It is still in my pocket
at the fair's end.
It is not only
suffering or grief
or even boredom
of which we are
offered more than
enough.

Kay Ryan

Further good advice for all of us. Spend that ticket!

TO YOU, PERHAPS YET UNBORN

It is night, and we are alone together; your head
Bends over the open book, your feeding eyes devour
The substance of my dream. Oh, sacred hour
That makes us one—you, fleeting, and I, already fled!

Here is my joy, here is my sorrow, my heart's rage,
Poured out for you. What tenderness brooding above you
Hallows these poems! I have made them all for you. I love you.
What love, what longing, my reader, speaks to you from
    this page!

John Hall Wheelock

THE CHEER

reader my friend, is in the words here, somewhere.
Frankly, I'd like to make you smile.
Words addressing evil won't turn evil back
but they can give heart.
The cheer is hidden in right words.

A great deal isn't right, as they say,
as they are lately at some pains to tell us.
Words have to speak about that.
They would be the less words
for saying *smile* when they should say *do*.
If you ask them *do what?*
they turn serious quick enough, but never unlovely.
And they will tell you what to do,
if you listen, if you want that.

Certainly good cheer has never been what's wrong,
though solemn people mistrust it.
Against evil, between evils, lovely words are right.
How absurd it would be to spin these noises out,
so serious that we call them poems,
if they couldn't make a person smile.
Cheer or courage is what they were all born in.
It's what they're trying to tell us, miming like that.
It's native to the words,
and what they want us always to know,
even when it seems quite impossible to do.

William Meredith

THE DEATH DEAL

Ever since that moment
when it first occurred
to me that I would die
(like everyone else on earth!)
I struggled against
this eventuality, but
never thought of
how I'd die, exactly,
until around thirty
I made a mental list:
hit by car, shot
in head by random ricochet,
crushed beneath boulder,
victim of gas explosion,
head banged hard
in fall from ladder,
vaporized in plane crash,
dwindling away with cancer,
and so on. I tried to think
of which I'd take
if given the choice,
and came up time
and time again with He died
in his sleep.
Now that I'm officially old,
though deep inside not
old officially or otherwise,
I'm oddly almost cheered

by the thought
that I might find out
in the not too distant future.
Now for lunch.

Ron Padgett

DAYS

Each one is a gift, no doubt,
mysteriously placed in your waking hand
or set upon your forehead
moments before you open your eyes.

Today begins cold and bright,
the ground heavy with snow
and the thick masonry of ice,
the sun glinting off the turrets of clouds.

Through the calm eye of the window
everything is in its place
but so precariously
this day might be resting somehow

on the one before it,
all the days of the past stacked high
like the impossible tower of dishes
entertainers used to build on stage.

No wonder you find yourself
perched on the top of a tall ladder
hoping to add one more.
Just another Wednesday,

you whisper,
then holding your breath,
place this cup on yesterday's saucer
without the slightest clink.

Billy Collins

ADVICE

Folks, I'm telling you,
birthing is hard
and dying is mean—
so get yourself
a little loving
in between.

Langston Hughes

ACKNOWLEDGMENTS

The editors wish to thank the following people for help and encouragement in bringing this book to fruition:

Gina Maccoby, Michael Pietsch, Megan Tingley, Frederick Courtright, Karen Landry, Jean Garnett, and members of the editorial staff of Little, Brown, whose attention to detail delighted our hearts.

Members of the Third Friday Poetry Reading Group, past and present, and in memory of Mary Coan, Phyllis Herman, Kay Langan, Jane Milliken, and Gail Wilson.

John Hopley and George, Gretchen, and John Hopley. Denny, Perry, Chuck, and Meg Hoberman, and in memory of Norman Hoberman.

And all of our families, friends, and colleagues whose enthusiasm for our project has carried us forward from that first germ of an idea to the volume you hold in your hands.

PERMISSIONS

Poems not credited here are in the public domain.

Marjorie Agosín, "Mi Estomago" ("My Belly"), translated by Cola Franzen, from *Women and Aging: An Anthology by Women,* edited by Jo Alexander. Copyright © 1986 by Marjorie Agosín. Used by permission of the author; Elizabeth Alexander, "Alice at One Hundred and Two" from *Women and Aging: An Anthology by Women,* edited by Jo Alexander. Copyright © 1986 by Elizabeth Alexander. Used by permission of the author; A. R. Ammons, "In View of the Fact" from *Bosh and Flapdoodle.* Copyright © 2005 by A. R. Ammons. "Gravelly Run" and "The City Limits" from *The Selected Poems, Expanded Edition.* Copyright © 1987, 1977, 1975, 1974, 1972, 1971, 1970, 1966, 1965, 1964, 1955 by A. R. Ammons. All used by permission of W. W. Norton & Company, Inc.; John Ashbery, "Fear of Death" from *Self-Portrait in a Convex Mirror.* Copyright © 1990 by John Ashbery. Used by permission of Viking Books, an imprint of Penguin Publishing Group, a division of Penguin Random House LLC and Carcanet Press, Ltd. All rights reserved; W. H. Auden, "Posthumous Letter to Gilbert White" and "After Reading a Child's Guide to Modern Physics" from *Collected Poems.* Copyright © 1976 by the Estate of W. H. Auden. Used by permission of Random House, an imprint and division of Penguin Random House LLC and Curtis Brown, Ltd. All rights reserved; Wendell Berry, "They," "The Burial of the Old," "Why," "Except," and "The Peace of Wild Things" from *New Collected Poems.* Copyright © 2012 by Wendell Berry. Reprinted by permission of Counterpoint; Elizabeth Bishop, "One Art" and "Sonnet" ("Caught—the bubble") from *The Complete Poems 1926–1979.* Copyright © 1979 by Elizabeth Bishop. Reprinted by

ABOUT THE POETS

AGOSÍN, MARJORIE (1955–)
Born in Chile, Agosín is a Chilean American who has written close to twenty books of poetry, fiction, and literary criticism. She has received Chilean government recognition for her activism on women's rights. She was also honored by the United Nations for her human rights work. Immigration and displacement are frequent themes in her poetry. She is a Spanish professor at Wellesley College, and her most recent collection is *Harbors of Light* (2016).

ALEXANDER, ELIZABETH (1962–)
Born in Harlem, New York City, Alexander is a poet, educator, and arts activist. She was raised primarily in Washington, DC, where her father was chair of the Equal Employment Opportunity Commission. She has taught at numerous universities, including Yale, where she was chair of the Department of African American Studies. She is currently president of the Andrew W. Mellon Foundation. At the 2009 presidential inauguration of Barack Obama, she recited her poem "Praise Song for the Day," written for the ceremony. She is author or co-author of fourteen books. Her memoir, *The Light of the World* (2015), was a finalist for the 2016 Pulitzer Prize for Poetry.

AMMONS, A. R. (1926–2001)
Twice a winner of a National Book Award (1973 and 1993), Ammons grew up in rural North Carolina during the Great Depression. He began writing while stationed on the battleship escort USS *Gunason* during World War II. Following the war and after gaining a university degree, he held various jobs, eventually becoming the Goldwin Smith Professor of English and poet-in-residence at Cornell University.

Recognized widely as a major American poet, Ammons once remarked, "I never dreamed of being a Poet poet. I think I always wanted to be an amateur poet." *A Coast of Trees* (1981) won the National Book Critics Circle Award.

ANACREON (C. 582–485 BC)

This Greek lyric poet was primarily a writer of hymns and drinking songs, written to be accompanied by the music of the lyre, a small harp. His principal themes include love and its disappointments, revelry, and the ordinary life of his fellow citizens.

ASHBERY, JOHN (1927–2017)

The recipient of many awards, including the 1976 Pulitzer Prize for his breakout collection *Self-Portrait in a Convex Mirror,* Ashbery published more than thirty volumes of poetry. Born in Rochester, New York, he was raised on a farm near Lake Ontario. While many find his poetry obscure, Ashbery said: "My poetry imitates or reproduces the way knowledge comes to me, which is by fits and starts...I don't think poetry arranged in neat patterns would reflect that situation. My poetry is disjunct, but then so is life." *John Ashbery: Collected Poems 1991–2000* was published in 2017.

AUDEN, W. H. (1907–1973)

One of the great twentieth-century poets, Auden combined a wide-ranging intelligence and a great command of the English language. He wrote poems in nearly every form. From the time he entered the University of Oxford, his talents were immediately apparent. In 1939 he and fellow poet Christopher Isherwood immigrated to the United States; he became a citizen in 1946. His works include plays, essays, and political commentary, many of them written in collaboration with fellow poets. His *Collected Poems* was published in 1976.

BERRY, WENDELL (1934–)

Whether he is writing poetry, essays, or fiction, Berry's overriding concern has been living in harmony with the earth. He has pursued his twin interests of agriculture and the environment while living on a farm in Kentucky near where he was born and raised. *The World-Ending Fire* (2017) is a volume of essays drawing parallels between how we treat the land and how we treat each other. *The Art of Loading Brush* came out in 2017 as well.

BISHOP, ELIZABETH (1911–1979)

While Bishop published only 101 poems during her lifetime, others have been published posthumously, and her audience has continued to grow. After an unsettled childhood—her father died during her first year and her mother was institutionalized when Bishop was five—she was raised by her grandparents. Her poetry has two major themes: close observation of the natural world and human grief and alienation. She also worked as a painter. Among her many honors were the 1956 Pulitzer Prize and the 1970 National Book Award for poetry. *Elizabeth Bishop: Prose, Poems, and Letters* was published in 2008.

BODENHEIM, MAXWELL (1892–1954)

A prominent literary personage first in Chicago and then in New York City, Bodenheim published nine books of poetry and thirteen novels during his lifetime. His success was later compromised by personal behavior during the Prohibition years. He ended his life as a vagrant. *My Life and Loves in Greenwich Village,* mostly ghostwritten, was published posthumously in 1954.

BOOTH, PHILIP (1925–2007)

Booth's ten volumes of poetry reflect a life lived primarily in New England. In direct language his writings express the everyday concerns of New Englanders and how they live simultaneously on the land and the coastline, both actually and metaphorically. His awards included the Poets' Prize for *Lifelines: Selected Poems 1950–1999.*

BORGES, JORGE LUIS (1899–1986)

A major figure in Spanish-language literature, Borges was a writer of short stories, essays, and poems as well as a translator. Born in Argentina, he moved with his family to Switzerland, where he attended college. He returned to Buenos Aires in 1921 and worked as a librarian, eventually becoming director of the National Public Library and a professor of English literature at the University of Buenos Aires. As his eyesight deteriorated (he became totally blind in his mid-fifties), he turned increasingly to writing poetry, as he could keep an entire work in progress in his mind. He wrote: "When I think of what I've lost, I ask, 'Who knows themselves better than the blind?'—for every thought becomes a tool." In 1961 he received the first Prix International, which he shared with Samuel Beckett. In 1962 two anthologies of his work came out in English: *Ficciones* and *Labyrinths*.

BROWNING, ROBERT (1812–1889)

Born in London, Browning is among the most important English authors of the Victorian era. His father's vast collection of six thousand books in a variety of languages had a great impact on him. Along with Alfred Tennyson and Dante Rossetti, he perfected the dramatic monologue. In 1845 he met the poet Elizabeth Barrett and married her the following year. They moved to Italy, where they lived until his death. His most famous poem is *The Ring and the Book*, a twenty-thousand-line poem in blank verse, published in twelve volumes from 1868 to 1869.

CARVER, RAYMOND (1938–1988)

Carver was born in Clatskanie, Oregon, and grew up in Yakima, Washington, where his father worked in a sawmill. Carver senior was a storyteller whose tales about himself, his father, and his grandfather influenced his son. Known more as a writer of fiction than as a poet, Carver helped revitalize the short story. He was a National Book Award finalist in 1977 for his story collection *Will You Please Be Quiet, Please?* and a Pulitzer Prize finalist for his story collection *Cathedral* in 1984. He published eight volumes of poetry, the last, *A New Path to the Waterfall,* posthumously in 1989.

CAVAFY, C. P. (1863–1933)

Cavafy, an Egyptian Greek poet born in Alexandria, is considered the most important poet of the twentieth century writing in Greek. Characterized as unique by most of his contemporaries, he was described by E. M. Forster, one of his British admirers, as standing at "a slight angle to the universe." Cavafy lived in Alexandria almost his entire life, first with his mother until she died and then for the last twenty-five years alone. Although he had little formal education, he was a keen student of Greek history and well-read in both English and French. *The Collected Poems of C. P. Cavafy: A New Translation,* translated by Aliki Barnstone, was published in 2007.

CLIFTON, LUCILLE (1936–2010)

An American poet, writer, and educator from Buffalo, New York, Clifton was twice a finalist for the Pulitzer Prize for Poetry. In 2000 she received a National Book Award for *Blessing the Boats: New and Selected Poems 1988–2000.* Her work explores the black female experience in all its aspects. It is recognized for being both concise and straightforward. As she noted: "I would like to be seen as a woman whose roots go back to Africa, who tried to honor being human." *The Collected Poems of Lucille Clifton 1965–2010* was published posthumously in 2012.

COLLINS, BILLY (1941–)

Born in New York City, Billy Collins was selected as the US Poet Laureate for 2001 to 2003. In 2016 he retired as a Distinguished Professor after almost fifty years of teaching at the City University of New York in the MFA program and at several other universities. His lighthearted, witty style, often covering underlying serious concerns, has made him one of the country's most popular poets. *The Rain in Portugal: Poems* was published in 2016.

CUMMINGS, E. E. (1894–1962)

Poet, essayist, and playwright, Cummings was born in Cambridge, Massachusetts. His experiments with poetic forms and diction resulted in a new kind of poetry. He is most known for his use of lowercase letters and his unconventional placement of words on the page; both contribute to the playful ambiguity of his poems. A revised and expanded edition of *E. E. Cummings: Complete Poems 1904–1962* was published in 2016.

DICKINSON, EMILY (1830–1886)

One of the greatest American poets, Dickinson was born and lived most of her life in Amherst, Massachusetts. Her brief poems pushed the boundaries of the poetic conventions of the time by introducing short lines and unusual capitalization, and using rhyme words with close but not identical sounds. Few of her poems were published until after her death, and even when published, they were often changed by early editors to meet conventional poetic norms. The wide-ranging subject matter in her work is a tribute to the extraordinary power of her imagination. The home where she lived in self-chosen seclusion and the room in which she wrote are now open to the public. *The Poems of Emily Dickinson: Reading Edition* was published in 2005.

DUFFY, CAROL ANN (1955–)

Born in Glasgow, Duffy is a poet and a playwright. She was named British Poet Laureate in 2009, and she is a professor of contemporary poetry at Manchester Metropolitan University. Her poems are often feminist in nature, speaking to the current concerns of women. Her most recent poems are about important historical events looked at from a female perspective. *The World's Wife* was published in 2007.

DUGAN, ALAN (1923–2003)

Dugan's first book of poetry, *Poems* (1961), won the Yale Series of Younger Poets award and went on to receive both a National Book Award and a Pulitzer Prize in 1962. He maintained his high writing standards throughout his career. His work centered on daily life with its recurring ups and downs, often leavened with a dry sense of humor. *Poems Seven: New and Complete Poetry* was published in 2001.

EBERHART, RICHARD (1904–2005)

Eberhart won the Pulitzer Prize for Poetry in 1966 for *Selected Poems 1930–1965* and the National Book Award for Poetry in 1977 for *Collected Poems 1930–1976*. As he was born and raised in Minnesota, many of his poems reflect a rural upbringing as well as his later work as a ship's hand. Interestingly, in his youth he was briefly a tutor to the son of the king of Siam. Eberhart taught at numerous colleges, including Dartmouth, where he became professor emeritus. He was widely admired for his style and his lyricism. *New and Selected Poems 1930–1990* was published in 1990.

EMERSON, RALPH WALDO (1803–1882)

Born in Boston, Emerson is a seminal American poet, essayist, and philosopher. His writings and lectures promoted the values of individualism and self-reliance. He was a leader of the transcendental movement with its core belief in the essential goodness of people and nature. He wrote: "To the attentive eye, each moment of the year has its own beauty, and in the same field, it beholds, every hour, a picture which was never seen before, and which will never be seen again." *Ralph Waldo Emerson: Collected Poems and Translations* was published by the Library of America in 1994.

EWART, GAVIN (1916–1995)

Ewart's first book, *Poems and Songs,* was published when he was only seventeen. He was born in London, and his active service during World War II interrupted his writing career. After the war he became an advertising copywriter and did not return to poetry until he reached his forties. He then published a number of popular collections of his own verse as well as edited numerous anthologies. *The Collected Ewart 1933–1980* was followed by *Collected Poems 1980–1990*.

FEINSTEIN, ELAINE (1930–)

Feinstein is an English poet, short-story writer, and playwright. Her Russian Jewish heritage places her in close accord with Russian poets of both the last and this century. Inspired by the poems of Maria Tsvetayeva, Feinstein commented that she wants "lines that come singing out of poems with a perfection of phrasing like lines of music." Among the other influences on her work are the writings of Ezra Pound and William Carlos Williams. Her volume *Cities* was published in 2010.

FROST, ROBERT (1874–1963)

Frost, born in San Francisco, moved to New England with his family after the early death of his father. This great American poet's work was first published in England. He won four Pulitzer Prizes, among countless other honors. Famously, at the 1961 inauguration of President Kennedy, after sunlight prevented him from reading his prepared remarks, he recited by heart his poem "The Gift Outright," which he had written twenty years earlier. At the time he was eighty-eight years old. *The Poetry of Robert Frost* was published in 1969.

GLÜCK, LOUISE (1943–)

Glück received the Pulitzer Prize for Poetry in 1993 for *The Wild Iris* and the National Book Award for Poetry in 2014 for *Faithful and Virtuous Night*. Born in New York City and raised on Long Island, Glück is considered one of the leading contemporary poets, her work often grouped with others of the confessional and subjective school. Her poems explore the darker aspects of life in straightforward and precise diction. She is writer-in-residence at Yale University and lives in Cambridge, Massachusetts. *Poems 1962–2012* was published in 2012.

GOLDBARTH, ALBERT (1948–)

American poet and essayist Goldbarth has twice won the National Book Critics Circle Award—for *Heaven and Earth: A Cosmology* (1991) and *Saving Lives* (2001)—the only poet to receive that honor two times. He received the Poetry Foundation Mark Twain Award for humorous poetry in 2008. A prolific writer, he has been described as one who can "see metaphor in almost any event" and as "a contemporary genius with...language." Goldbarth is a fellow of both the National Endowment for the Arts and the John Simon Guggenheim Memorial Foundation. He is the Adele Davis Distinguished Professor of Humanities at Wichita State University, where he has taught for many years. *The Kitchen Sink: New and Selected Poems: 1972–2007* was published in 2007.

GREGER, DEBORA (1949–)

A graduate of the Iowa Writers' Workshop, Greger has published numerous poetry books, receiving grants from the Guggenheim Foundation and the National Endowment for the Arts. An artist working in collage as well as a poet, she recommended that her writing students look to the visual arts for ideas. Prior to her retirement, she was a professor of English and creative writing at the University of Florida. She lives in Gainesville, Florida, and Cambridge, England, with her longtime partner and collaborator, the poet William Logan.

HAN YU (D. 824)

Han Yu was a Chinese poet, writer, and government official of the Tang dynasty whose significance in Asia is comparable to that of Dante or Shakespeare in the West. The end of his government service came as a result of his writings against the growing Buddhist influence in his country. In its place, he strongly supported Confucianism and developed a form of it that encompassed political action.

HARRISON, JEFFREY (1957–)

Harrison was born in Cincinnati, Ohio. His poems are personal, often dealing with the ordinary. He attended Columbia University and now lives in Massachusetts. Speaking of his writing, he notes: "I like to have my desk up against a window so I can daydream...but I don't have a routine, a special time to write." About the poet's role, he says: "Perhaps honesty is the prime responsibility—honesty about oneself and about what the world is like." *Into Daylight,* published in 2014, is his most recent book of poetry.

HARRISON, JIM (1937–2016)

A prolific American poet, novelist, and essayist of the West, Harrison claimed that of all his writings, poetry meant the most to him. His awards include a Guggenheim Fellowship and election into the American Academy of Arts and Letters. Two of his novellas were made into the movie *Legends of the Fall* (1994). His last book of poetry, *Dead Man's Float,* was published shortly before his death.

Heaney, Seamus (1939–2013)

Born in Northern Ireland, the first of nine children, Heaney was awarded the Nobel Prize in Literature in 1995 "for works of lyrical beauty and ethical depth." Both poet and playwright, he lived part-time in the United States from 1981 to 2006, when he taught at Harvard and was poet-in-residence as well. He also was a poetry professor at Oxford. His work was strongly influenced by his upbringing in Ireland, with its tension between the rural and the industrial and its troubled history. *New and Selected Poems 1988–2013* came out in 2014. His *Collected Poems,* published in 2009, is a multi-volume CD set of Heaney reading all his published poems. Only the poems in his final book, *Human Chain* (2010), are not included. In the title poem of the book he writes: "A letting go which will not come again. / Or it will, once. And for all."

Herbert, Zbigniew (1924–1998)

Herbert was a Polish poet, essayist, and moralist, and one of the best known and frequently translated post–World War II writers. His work has been nominated for the Nobel Prize in literature. Trained as an economist, he became active in the Resistance during the war, and as a young man he published only a few of his poems in the underground press. After the war, he traveled widely, eventually returning to Warsaw, where he died. In 2013 the Polish government established the Zbigniew Herbert International Literary Award in honor of his legacy. His *Collected Poems, 1956–1998,* edited by Alissa Valles, was published in 2000.

Hirshfield, Jane (1953–)

Hirshfield was born and raised in Manhattan and now lives in the San Francisco area. After graduating from Princeton, she studied at the Zen Center in San Francisco. About poetry she writes: "Poems carry shimmer, multiplicity, undertow, mystery, kites of meaning, and feeling so elusive they cannot be seen, yet they tauten the string that holds them." Her poems, apparently simple on the surface, become more complex on further reading. She has taught at colleges and universities from California to Alaska. *The Beauty* was published in 2015.

Hoagland, Tony (1953–2018)

Born at Fort Bragg, North Carolina, where his father was an army surgeon, Hoagland had a peripatetic childhood and adolescence, living in Ethiopia, Hawaii, and throughout the continental United States. Poetry provided him with an anchor. "It was the only thing that stayed constant in my life," he said. He studied at Williams College and earned an undergraduate degree from the University of Iowa; later he got an MFA from the University of Arizona. *Sweet Ruin,* his first poetry collection, was published in 1992. He went on to publish six more poetry books as well as a number of chapbooks and essay collections. He was a champion of accessible and humorous poetry, but also, as critic Dwight Garner wrote: "His erudite comic poems are backloaded with heartache and longing." His last book, published in 2018, was *Priest Turned Therapist Treats Fear of God.*

HOBERMAN, MARY ANN (1930–)

Hoberman, the former Children's Poet Laureate (2008–2011), was born in Stamford, Connecticut. She graduated from Smith College and, thirty years later, received a master's degree from Yale University. She is the critically acclaimed author of more than forty books for children, including *A House Is a House for Me* (1978), winner of a National Book Award. She also received the 2003 Award for Excellence in Poetry for Children given by the National Council of Teachers of English. One hundred of her favorite poems are collected in *The Llama Who Had No Pajama* (1998). Other popular titles include *The Seven Silly Eaters* (1997) and the *New York Times* bestselling series You Read to Me, I'll Read to You. Her latest children's book is *The Sun Shines Everywhere* (Little, Brown, 2019). She lives in Connecticut.

HOLLANDER, JOHN (1929–2013)

One of America's foremost contemporary poets and literary critics, Hollander was a member of the American Academy of Arts and Letters, a MacArthur Fellow, and Poet Laureate of Connecticut. He taught at several universities, including Connecticut College, Hunter College, and Yale University, where he served as Sterling Professor of English. Hollander emphasized the importance of hearing poetry read out loud: "A good poem satisfies...informs you and entertains you." Some of his poems were set to music by Milton Babbitt, Elliott Carter, and others. *A Draft of Light* (2008) was his last volume of poetry.

HOPKINS, GERARD MANLEY (1844–1889)

Most poems written by Hopkins, one of the greatest Victorian poets, were not published during his lifetime. Born in Stratford, England, the eldest of nine children, he grew up in a well-to-do and accomplished

Anglican family. He first wanted to be a painter but turned to the study of classics and writing poetry while attending Oxford. In 1866 he converted to Roman Catholicism. This act estranged him from his family and many of his friends. Torn between his Jesuit religious vows and his poetic talent, he gave up writing poems almost entirely for seven years, but eventually he came to the conclusion there was no conflict between the two pursuits. Hopkins's importance as a poet centers on his unconventional uses of meter and rhythmic structure, drawing on the Anglo-Saxon tradition in English poetry as exemplified in *Beowulf*. He called his method "sprung rhythm." A good introduction to his work is *Gerard Manley Hopkins: The Major Works,* published by Oxford University Press.

HUGHES, LANGSTON (1902–1967)

A leading American poet, novelist, playwright, and social activist, Hughes was born in Joplin, Missouri, and moved to New York City after growing up in the Midwest. His father left the family soon after Hughes's birth and moved to Mexico to escape the pervasive racism in the United States. While his mother worked, Hughes was raised primarily by his maternal grandmother, who passed on to him the black oral tradition and a sense of racial pride. In his autobiography he wrote: "I was unhappy for a long time, and very lonesome, living with my grandmother. Then it was that books began to happen to me, and I began to believe in nothing but books and the wonderful world in books—where if people suffered, they suffered in beautiful language, not in monosyllables, as we did in Kansas." Hughes's literary production is enormous: more than fifty books of poetry, novels and short-story collections, plays, nonfiction books, and books for children. *The Collected Poems of Langston Hughes* was published in 1994.

JAMES, CLIVE (1939–2019)

Born in Australia, James lived and worked in England since 1962. His father was imprisoned by the Japanese during World War II and died in an airplane crash shortly after his release. James, an only child, was raised by his mother, a factory worker. After he immigrated to England, he worked briefly at various jobs before attending the University of Cambridge, where he studied English literature. He was a television, literary, and cultural critic for various periodicals, and his work was gathered in many collections. He also published four novels, five memoirs, six epics, and seven collections of poetry. The latest, *Injury Time* (2017), dealt with his illness. He passed away in 2019.

KNOTT, BILL (1940–2014)

Knott was a maverick whose poems were often self-published and whose first collection was published under a pseudonym, Saint Geraud, purportedly that of a poet who had committed suicide prior to publication. Knott was an orphan and worked on a farm in Michigan with his uncle. After serving in the army, he taught for many years at Emerson College in Boston. *The Unsubscriber* was published in 2004. *I Am Flying into Myself: Selected Poems 1960–2014* was compiled by the poet Thomas Lux and came out in 2017.

KOOSER, TED (1939–)

A popular American poet and the thirteenth US Poet Laureate, Kooser was one of the first to be chosen for the honor from the Great Plains. In 2005 he received the Pulitzer Prize for Poetry for *Delights and Shadows*. Before his retirement, Kooser was vice president of an insurance company, writing before work every morning. A professor of English at the University of Nebraska–Lincoln, Kooser lives in rural Nebraska. His most recent book is *Kindest Regards: New and Selected Poems* (2018).

KUNITZ, STANLEY (1905–2006)

Born in Worcester, Massachusetts, Kunitz was the youngest of three children of Russian Jewish immigrants. Six weeks before he was born, his father committed suicide, and his mother raised the family alone. At fifteen he moved out of his home and became a butcher's assistant. He graduated summa cum laude and earned an MA from Harvard. After serving in World War II as a conscientious objector, he taught at various colleges and universities, eventually becoming a professor of writing for eighteen years at Columbia University's School of the Arts. Kunitz was an avid gardener and for many years maintained a seaside garden in Provincetown, Massachusetts. His poetry, often very personal, uses flowers and other natural phenomena both descriptively and metaphorically. Kunitz was the recipient of numerous awards, including a Pulitzer Prize in 1959 for his *Selected Poems 1928–1958* and a National Book Award in 1995 for *Passing Through*. That he was still publishing poems one hundred years after his birth is evidence of his amazingly long writing career. *The Collected Poems* was published in 2000.

LARKIN, PHILIP (1922–1985)

A British poet and novelist, Larkin gained his undergraduate degree from the University of Oxford. For thirty years he worked as university librarian at the University of Hull while concurrently writing his poetry. Larkin also wrote two novels, criticism, essays, and jazz reviews. Although he published only four small volumes of poetry over his lifetime, he was extremely popular. In 1975 critic Alan Brownjohn wrote that Larkin produced "the most technically brilliant and resonantly beautiful, profoundly disturbing yet appealing and approachable, body of verse of any English poet in the last twenty-five years." *The Whitsun Weddings* (1964) and *High Windows* (1974) are his two last books of poetry, the latter containing one of his best-known poems, "This Be the Verse." *Philip Larkin: Collected Poems,* edited by Anthony Thwaite, was published in 1988.

LAWRENCE, D. H. (1885–1930)

In his short life Lawrence wrote prolifically in many genres: novels, short stories, plays, essays, travel books, translations, literary criticism, and poetry. He was the youngest of four children, his father an uneducated miner, his mother a former teacher who had to perform factory work to help support the family. From an early age Lawrence escaped the tensions at home by roaming in the hilly open countryside, and the natural world was one of his primary concerns in all his writing. He earned a teaching certificate while working on his first poems and stories. Lawrence's controversial opinions on human sexuality and the rigid conformity brought on by modern industrialization made him a pariah in England, and he left shortly after World War I to travel the world, returning to England only for brief visits. E. M. Forster, in an obituary, called him "the greatest imaginative novelist of our generation," and this evaluation has become widely accepted in the years since his death. Of Lawrence's twelve novels, *Sons and Lovers* (1913) and *Lady Chatterley's Lover* (1928) are among the best known. His poetry was gathered into the collection *Complete Poems* (Vivian de Sola Pinto and Warren F. Roberts, editors) in 1994.

LEE, LI-YOUNG (1957–)

Lee is an American poet born in Indonesia to Chinese political exiles. The family arrived in the United States in 1964. Lee began writing poetry while attending the University of Pittsburgh. He has taught at various universities, including Northwestern University and the University of Iowa. Strongly influenced by classic Chinese poets, his writing has a distinct spiritual cast. His five books include *Behind My Eyes* (2008) and *The Undressing* (2018).

LE GUIN, URSULA K. (1929–2018)

Born in Berkeley, California, Le Guin came from an intellectual background. Both her parents were anthropologists; her mother was also the author of the well-known *Ishi in Two Worlds,* a biography of the last known member of the Yahi tribe. Although known primarily as a writer of science fiction and fantasy, Le Guin published numerous books of poetry; the last one, *So Far So Good,* came out just before she died. One critic, David Naiman, commented: "The through line of Le Guin's career is how she attends to language, even in her prose, with the sensibility of a poet." Her poems, unlike her fiction, deal with the world as we know it. Le Guin championed many causes, especially as concerned freedom of speech, environmentalism, and peace. Her many honors included dozens of awards for science fiction and fantasy and the Medal for Distinguished Contribution to American Letters by the National Book Foundation in 2014. *No Time to Spare: Thinking About What Matters* was published in 2017.

LERMAN, ELEANOR (1952–)

Lerman was born and grew up in New York City. At eighteen she struck out on her own and moved to Greenwich Village, where she found a job sweeping up in a harpsichord factory. This took place in what she describes as "the psychedelic days," and she soon fell in with a group of artists who encouraged her as a poet. She submitted her first book, *Armed Love,* to Wesleyan University Press, and it was published in 1973 and nominated for a National Book Award. She was twenty-one. While the book was generally well reviewed, the poet X. J. Kennedy in the *New York Times* described it as "XX rated." The resulting notoriety frightened her, and although she published another book shortly after, she eventually left New York, married, and gave up writing. After a twenty-five-year hiatus, she began to write poems again. Since then, she has published four more books of poetry, along with several novels and short-story collections. Her most recent book of poems is *Strange Life* (2014).

Levertov, Denise (1923–1997)

Although born and raised in England, Levertov is considered an American poet. Levertov's mother was Welsh, and her father was a Russian Hasidic Jew who converted to Christianity and became an Anglican priest. Growing up with such a mixed heritage, Levertov always felt herself special: "[I knew] before I was ten that I was an artist-person and I had a destiny." When she was twenty-four, she married the American writer Mitchell Goodman and moved to the United States. In 1955 she became a US citizen. Levertov published two dozen books of poetry as well as essays, letters, criticism, and translations. She was a committed feminist and very active politically during both the Vietnam and the Iraq wars. For much of her writing career she included political themes in her poetry, but eventually she concentrated on the religious and mystical concerns that had also preoccupied her throughout her life. *Selected Poems* was published in 2002.

Lewis, Janet (1899–1998)

In the course of a century-long life, Lewis published her poetry, fiction, and opera librettos in almost every decade. Born in Chicago, she graduated from the University of Chicago and married the poet Yvor Winters in 1926. She began as an imagist poet grouped with William Carlos Williams and Marianne Moore. After she moved to Los Altos, California, where she lived until her death, she devoted most of her energy to raising her two children and providing a hospitable retreat for her husband's admiring students. She taught at both Stanford University and the University of California, Berkeley. Her poems, quiet and well crafted, speak to the reader with integrity and depth. The last of her ten books of poetry, *The Selected Poems of Janet Lewis*, was published posthumously in 2000.

Louie, Diane (1953–)

Louie was born in Newfoundland and grew up in Connecticut. She has degrees from Oberlin College and the Iowa Writers' Workshop (for both poetry and fiction), where she held a Teaching-Writing Fellowship. Her book of prose poems, *Fractal Shores,* is a winner of the National Poetry Series. She currently lives in Paris, France, with her partner, a research scientist.

LYNCH, THOMAS (1948–)

Lynch is an American poet and essayist, as well as a professional under-taker who took over his father's funeral home in Milford, Michigan, in 1974. An adjunct professor of creative writing at the University of Michigan, Ann Arbor, he received an American Book Award for his collection of essays *The Undertaking: Life Studies from the Dismal Trade* (1997). He has published five books of poetry, his latest being *The Sin-Eater: A Breviary*.

MACLEISH, ARCHIBALD (1892–1982)

MacLeish, writer and statesman, was born in Glencoe, Illinois, and attended Yale University, writing for college magazines and winning the university's Prize Poem award in 1915. He served in France in World War I and published his first poetry collection, *Tower of Ivory,* in 1917. He then attended Harvard Law School. But after a few years he relin-quished his legal career to move to Paris with his young family and write poetry. Returning to the United States, he was appointed by Pres-ident Franklin D. Roosevelt as Librarian of Congress, the first of the many governmental posts he occupied until the end of World War II. He returned to academia in 1949 as a professor at Harvard University. Toggling between writing and public service throughout his long life, he left a lasting legacy in both areas. He won two Pulitzer Prizes for his poetry and one for his play *J.B.* His *New and Collected Poems 1917–1976* was published in 1976.

MAJ, BRONISLAW (1953–)

Maj is a major Polish poet, critic, translator, and essayist currently liv-ing in Kraków. He received his PhD in the humanities from the Jagiel-lonian University and published his first book of poetry in 1980. He currently teaches Polish literature at the Jagiellonian University. As yet none of his books have been translated into English.

MEREDITH, WILLIAM (1919–2007)

Born in New York City, Meredith began to write poetry in college. His first book, *Love Letters from an Impossible Land,* published when he was twenty-five, won the Yale Series of Younger Poets award. He served as a US Army Air Force pilot in both World War II and the Korean War. He taught at the college level for many years, eventually becoming a professor of English at Connecticut College. In 1983 he suffered a stroke, which caused expressive aphasia, affecting his ability to speak. Unable to teach or write poetry, he ended his teaching career. After years of extensive rehabilitation he began composing poems again, while continuing his avocation of arborist on his Connecticut farm. The recipient of many honors and awards, including the 1988 Pulitzer Prize for Poetry, he also was US Poet Laureate. *Effort at Speech: New and Selected Poems* won the 1997 National Book Award for Poetry.

MERWIN, W. S. (1927–2019)

Merwin was born in New York City and grew up in New Jersey and Pennsylvania. After attending Princeton University, he moved to Spain, at one point serving as tutor to the poet Robert Graves's son. In 1952 W. H. Auden chose Merwin's first book, *A Mask for Janus,* as winner of the Yale Series of Younger Poets Competition. Merwin was also a playwright, translator, and editor. Over the years his poetry became less formal and controlled, its subject matter more spiritual and devoted to the natural world. Merwin was a practicing Buddhist, and in 1976 he moved to Hawaii to study with the Zen master Robert Aitken. In 2010 he and his wife co-founded the nonprofit Merwin Conservancy on the island of Maui to preserve their home and property, which contains one of the largest collections of rare palm trees in the world. Merwin received many honors, including a National Book Award for *Migration: New and Selected Poems* (2005) and two Pulitzer Prizes, for *The Carrier of Ladders* (1970) and *The Shadow of Sirius* (2008).

MILLAY, EDNA ST. VINCENT (1892–1950)

The third woman to receive the Pulitzer Prize for Poetry (1923), Millay was one of the most popular and respected poets in the United States for much of her career. The subjects of her always progressive writing ranged from the political to the personal (and strongly feminist). She was also a gifted writer of sonnets and a poetic playwright: *Aria da capo* is her most experimental play. In *A Few Figs from Thistles* (1920), her mocking sense of humor makes its appearance: "My candle burns at both ends; / It will not last the night; / But ah, my foes, and oh, my friends—/ It gives a lovely light!" *The Selected Poetry of Edna St. Vincent Millay* (Modern Library Classics edition) was published in 2002.

Milosz, Czeslaw (1911–2004)

Awarded the Nobel Prize in Literature in 1980, Milosz is considered one of the twentieth century's major poets, both in his native Poland and in the world. A prolific writer in many genres, he was also an important political figure in Poland after World War II. His anti-Stalinist views eventually led him to defect to the West, first to Paris and then to the United States, where he became a citizen in 1979. From 1961 to 1998 he was a professor of Slavic languages and literature at the University of California, Berkeley. He was fluent in many languages and translated much of his own poetry into English, often working with his colleague the American poet Robert Hass. After the fall of the Iron Curtain, he lived part-time in Kraków. The critic Terrence Des Pres commented: "Milosz deals in his poetry with the central issues of our time: the impact of history upon moral being, the search for ways to survive spiritual ruin in a ruined world." *New and Collected Poems 1931–2001* was published in 2001 and reprinted in paperback in 2017.

Moore, Marianne (1887–1972)

Moore was born in Missouri and grew up in Pennsylvania. Her parents separated before she was born, and Moore never met her father. Moore graduated from Bryn Mawr College, where she wrote poetry for the college's literary magazines. After studying at a commercial college, she and her mother moved to New York City in 1918. She started working at the New York Public Library in 1921. At that time she was part of the imagist group of poets, and her first book, *Poems,* was published in London without her permission. In regard to her poetic style, she wrote of her preference for "the unaccented rhyme, the movement of the poem musically is more important than the conventional look of lines upon the page." She would place exact rhymes within rather than at the ends of her lines and varied the shape of her stanzas according to the poem. In 1952 Moore's *Collected Poems* won a National Book Award and a Pulitzer Prize, and prior to that, in 1951, the Bollingen Prize for Poetry. By then Moore had become a quasi-celebrity, speaking at colleges across the country, a striking figure in her tricorn hat and black cape. She was a great baseball fan and threw out the opening pitch at Yankee Stadium in 1968. Her *Complete Poems* was reissued in 1994.

MORLEY, HILDA (1916–1998)

Born in New York City to Russian Jewish immigrants, Morley was a precocious child, sending poems to W. B. Yeats, who encouraged her in her writing. At fifteen she moved to Haifa, Palestine, with her mother; later she studied at the University of London. When the bombing of London began, she returned to the United States and married painter Eugene Morley. Through him she met many of the New York abstract expressionists, whose art had a major influence on her poems. The couple divorced a few years later, and in 1952 she married the German composer Stefan Wolpe. They both taught at Black Mountain College in North Carolina. Morley did not publish her first book, *A Blessing Outside Us,* until 1976, when she was sixty. For many years before that, she had been the primary caretaker of her husband, who died of Parkinson's disease in 1972. Morley had been praised by many of her contemporaries for her skill and insight; they regretted that her work had not found a wider audience. The poet Hayden Carruth wrote of one of her poems: "How simple the language is, not a rhetorical gesture, not an unnecessary adjective, yet heightened by interweaving lines, cadences, and tones, by urgency of feeling and fineness of perception." Morley published six collections, the last of which was *The Turning* (1998).

NASH, OGDEN (1902–1971)

Ogden Nash is a national treasure
Who has given his readers much pleasure.
Though his rhythms are often erratic
And his rhyming at times problematic,
Every line of his verse,
Be it prolix or terse,
Has elicited joy without measure
(And it earned him a nice wad of cash).
So three cheers for our great Ogden Nash!

NORRIS, GUNILLA (1939–)

Norris is the author of two books of poetry: *Learning from the Angel* and *Joy Is the Thinnest Layer.* The latter won the Nautilus gold medal for the best book of poetry in 2017. She is also the author of eleven books on the spirituality of the everyday. The most recent is *Great Love in Little Ways: Reflections on the Power of Kindness* (2019). A mother and grandmother, Norris has been a psychotherapist in private practice for more than forty-five years and has felt privileged to accompany many people on their journeys to growth, healing, and spiritual connectedness.

OSTRIKER, ALICIA (1937–)

Born in Brooklyn, New York, Ostriker is a poet, critic, teacher, and outspoken feminist. A writer since childhood, she did her doctoral dissertation on the work of William Blake. She has taught at Rutgers University since 1972 and is now professor emerita of English. Her poetry and criticism deal with social justice, her Jewish feminist identity, and personal growth. She has received fellowships from the National Endowment for the Arts (1976–77), the Rockefeller Foundation (1982), and the Guggenheim Foundation (1984–85). *The Crack in Everything* (1996) was a National Book Award finalist. Her most recent book is *Waiting for the Light* (2017).

PADGETT, RON (1942–)

Padgett is a poet, editor, and translator as well as a fiction writer and memoirist. He has also collaborated with various artists in works in the surrealist and dadaist traditions. Born in Tulsa, Oklahoma, he cofounded a literary review while he was still in high school. After graduating from Columbia University in 1960, a Fulbright award enabled him to spend a year in Paris studying French poetry. He has taught at and directed the Poetry Project at St. Mark's Church and been publications director at the Teachers and Writers Collaborative, both in New York City. *How Long* was a finalist for the Pulitzer Prize for Poetry in 2011, and *Collected Poems* won the Los Angeles Times Book Prize in 2013.

PALEY, GRACE (1922–2007)

While known primarily for her short stories and political activism, Paley published three volumes of poetry, beginning in her sixties. Born in New York City, she was the daughter of immigrants from Ukraine. She attended Hunter College and The New School, taught at Sarah Lawrence College, and was a co-founder of the Teachers and Writers Collaborative in New York. As an antinuclear pacifist, she demonstrated against the Vietnam War and in 1978 was part of a peace mission to Hanoi, trying to gain the release of prisoners of war. Her poems are direct and honest, informed by her warmth and humor, her love of family, and her deep human understanding. Among other honors, she received a Guggenheim Fellowship for Fiction in 1961. Her *Begin Again: Collected Poems* was published in 2000.

PASTAN, LINDA (1932–)

Born and raised in New York City, Pastan has lived since then in Maryland, where she served as Poet Laureate from 1991 to 1995. She won the *Mademoiselle* poetry prize while attending Radcliffe College (Sylvia Plath was the runner-up). Her poetry deals in a deceptively simple way with profound themes, both domestic and existential. She taught at the Bread Loaf Writers' Conference for twenty years. Her honors include the Dylan Thomas Award and the Ruth Lilly Poetry Prize in 2003. Of her recent book *Insomnia* (2015), she says she chose the title "because the word conjures for me a struggle with consciousness itself as well as a struggle with the looming dark, just outside the window" (*Paris Review* interview, January 6, 2006).

PEACOCK, MOLLY (1947–)

Poet, essayist, and biographer, Peacock was born in Buffalo, New York. She graduated from Harpur College (Binghamton University) and earned an MA from Johns Hopkins University. A former president of the Poetry Society of America, she inaugurated the Poetry in Motion program, which displays poems on New York City's subways and buses. She has taught at many universities and has published seven books of poetry. A dual citizen of the United States and Canada, she now lives in Toronto. She has been recognized by the National Endowment for the Arts and the Woodrow Wilson Foundation. Her latest book is *Analyst* (2017).

PLUTZIK, HYAM (1911–1962)

Plutzik was born in Brooklyn, New York, and raised in rural Connecticut. The son of Russian Jewish immigrants, he did not learn English until he was seven, when he began school in a one-room schoolhouse. A graduate of Trinity College in Hartford, Connecticut, he later studied at Yale, where he twice won the university's Cook prize for the best unpublished poem. After serving in the army during World War II, he became a professor at the University of Rochester for the rest of his career. Summing up his feelings about poetry, he wrote in an autobiographical essay: "I once looked at poetry as little more than beautiful language. Later, it was a way of communicating the nuances of the world. More recently I have begun to look at poetry as the great synthesizer, the humanizer of knowledge." Three of his four books of poetry were finalists for the Pulitzer Prize, including *Horatio* (1961), a long narrative poem in which Horatio fulfills Hamlet's dying plea "to tell my story." *Hyam Plutzik: The Collected Poems* was published in 1987.

PONSOT, MARIE (1921–2019)

Born in Brooklyn, New York, Ponsot graduated from St. Joseph's College for Women there and earned an MA from Columbia University in seventeeth-century literature. After World War II she went to Paris, married, and had a daughter. Returning to the United States, she had six sons before her divorce. Remarkably she wrote much of her poetry while raising her seven children mostly on her own. She translated many children's books from the French and was an English professor at Queens College in New York until her retirement in 1991. Her own books include *The Bird Catcher* (1998), winner of the National Book Critics Circle Award for Poetry, and *Springing: New and Selected Poems* (2002), a *New York Times* "notable book of the year."

POULTON, KATHIAN

Poulton teaches kindergarten in Columbus, Ohio. Her publications include education-related articles and an occasional poem or book review.

RAINE, KATHLEEN (1908–2003)

English poet Raine both heard and memorized poetry from her earliest childhood and was soon composing it herself. She studied the natural sciences in college, and her poems address the interface between science and spirituality. Also a scholar and critic, she published multiple works on Blake and Yeats along with sixteen books of her own poetry. Her first book of poems, *Stone and Flower,* came out in 1943; her last, *The Collected Poems of Kathleen Raine,* in 2000. She won the Queen's Gold Medal for Poetry in 1992.

RANDALL, MARGARET (1936–)

Randall is a writer, photographer, and academic. Born in New York City, she lived for many years in Spain, Mexico, Cuba, and Nicaragua, and also spent time in North Vietnam. During the 1950s she was connected with both the Beats and the abstract expressionists. Because of her political and feminist views, she often came into conflict with US authorities and faced deportation in 1984. After a five-year legal battle, she won her case. She now resides with her wife, the painter Barbara Byers, in New Mexico. Her most recent poetry collection is *Time's Language: Selected Poems 1959–2018.*

RICH, ADRIENNE (1929–2012)

Poet, essayist, and feminist, Rich was one of the leading American literary voices of the later twentieth century. Born in Baltimore, Maryland, she was encouraged by her parents to excel in her studies; she fulfilled their ambitions when she was chosen in 1950 by W. H. Auden for the Yale Series of Younger Poets award. But she soon outgrew her early formalist work and moved toward a more radical approach in both style and content. She was at the forefront of the feminist, lesbian, and antiwar movements from the sixties onward. Among her many honors was a National Book Award in 1974 for *Diving into the Wreck.* Her last collection was *Tonight No Poetry Will Serve: Poems 2007–2010.*

ROETHKE, THEODORE (1908–1963)

Born in Saginaw, Michigan, Roethke spent much of his time in his father's greenhouse, and natural themes play a large part in his poetry. In a letter to the poet Babette Deutsch he wrote that the greenhouse "is my symbol for the whole of life, a womb, a heaven-on-earth." Despite problems with alcohol and bouts of manic depression, he became one of America's leading poets and an important influence on poets of the next generation. *The Waking* (1953) won the Pulitzer Prize. *The Far Field* was his last book of poems, published posthumously in 1964.

RUMI, JALAL AL-DIN (1207–1273)

This thirteenth-century Persian mystic, poet, and scholar has been widely popular throughout the Middle East and Asia for seven centuries. While the actual facts of his birthplace and travels are in question, it is believed that as a young man he fled with his family to Turkey to avoid the armies of Genghis Khan. He became a leader of a sect of dervishes, Sufi holy men. His book *The Shams* is considered one of the great works of Persian literature. Primarily through poet Coleman Barks's translations, Rumi has become one of the most popular poets in the United States. Barks has written: "He wants us to be more alive, to wake up...He wants us to see our beauty, both in the mirror and in each other."

Ryan, Kay (1945–)

A lifelong Californian, Kay Ryan is a true original. Her crisp, compact poems have delighted readers with their witty turns of phrase and unexpected rhymes. For many years she taught English at her local community college in Marin County. She served two terms as US Poet Laureate (from 2008 to 2010) and in 2011 was awarded both a MacArthur Fellowship and the Pulitzer Prize for Poetry for her collection *The Best of It: New and Selected Poems*.

Snodgrass, W. D. (1926–2009)

Snodgrass was born in Pennsylvania, served in World War II, and then attended the University of Iowa. His first book, *Heart's Needle* (1959), won the Pulitzer Prize for Poetry. Its frankly autobiographical subject matter, about losing his daughter in a divorce case, influenced other confessional poets like Sylvia Plath and Robert Lowell. Snodgrass published more than thirty books of poetry, criticism, and translations, and taught at various colleges for forty years.

Stafford, William (1914–1993)

Poet and pacifist, Stafford got a relatively late start in publishing. He was in his forties when his first book came out in 1960, but he made up for lost time when his second book, *Traveling Through the Dark* (1962), won a National Book Award. A native of Kansas, he was a conscientious objector in World War II and did his alternative service in forestry in the west. The quiet and peace of the wilderness and living in harmony with nature became the moral touchstones of his poetry. Stafford eventually published fifty-seven volumes of poetry, along with criticism and a book of essays, *Writing the Australian Crawl: Views on the Writer's Vocation* (1978). *Ask Me: 100 Essential Poems* (2013) contains many of his most popular poems.

Stevens, Wallace (1879–1955)

One of America's great modernist poets, Stevens was born in Reading, Pennsylvania. He grew up in a home filled with books and, by the time he got to Harvard College, was an active writer. Unlike most of his poet peers, however, he did not go on to teach but instead briefly practiced law, then moved to Hartford, Connecticut, and spent the rest of his working life as an insurance executive. This choice worked well for him: steady and lucrative employment allowed him sufficient time to produce a large body of outstanding poems. While he was considered a difficult poet, his combination of aesthetic and philosophical subject matter expressed in extraordinary language has appealed to a wide variety of critics and readers. Among his honors were the Bollingen Prize for Poetry (1949), the National Book Award for Poetry (1951 and 1955), and the Pulitzer Prize for Poetry (1955). *The Collected Poems of Wallace Stevens* (1954) and *Collected Poetry and Prose* (Library of America, 1997) contain most of his work.

SUTPHEN, JOYCE (1949–)

Born and educated in Minnesota, Sutphen teaches British literature and creative writing at Gustavus Adolphus College in St. Peter, Minnesota. She is currently serving as the state's second Poet Laureate. She has published five books of poetry; her latest is *Modern Love and Other Myths* (2015).

SWENSON, MAY (1913–1989)

Born in Logan, Utah, to Swedish immigrant parents, Swenson was the eldest of ten children, all of whom spoke English as a second language. As a poet, she delighted in wordplay and was particularly interested in nature and scientific discovery. She published ten books of poetry during her lifetime and received numerous awards and honors, including a MacArthur Fellowship in 1987. Her *Collected Poems* (Library of America) came out in 2013.

SZYMBORSKA, WISLAWA (1923–2012)

A Polish poet, Szymborska was largely unknown in the West until she won the Nobel Prize in Literature in 1996. Her poems are often ironic and frequently deal with political and philosophical themes. She also wrote popular essays and stories. *Poems New and Collected* (1998), translated by Stanislaw Baranczak and Clare Cavanagh, won the PEN Translation Prize.

THOMAS, DYLAN (1914–1953)

One of the great Welsh poets (but writing in English), Thomas was born in Swansea, Wales. Some of his most famous poems were published while he was still in his teens. A masterful performer of his highly rhythmic and musical works, he visited the United States in

1950 and embarked on the first of a series of wildly popular readings at colleges and art centers. However, his unpredictable behavior and drinking problem worsened, and he died prematurely at thirty-nine. His many books and recordings, in both poetry and prose, include his *Collected Poems* (1952) and *A Child's Christmas in Wales* (1954).

TRANSTRÖMER, TOMAS (1931–2015)

Tranströmer is a world-famous Swedish poet whose work has been translated into more than fifty languages. His poems deal with spiritual and natural themes, often informed by the austere beauty of the Swedish landscape. After suffering a stroke in 1990 and losing his power of speech, he continued to write poetry and was awarded the Nobel Prize in Literature in 2011. His *Great Enigma: New Collected Poems* was published in 2006.

VONNEGUT, KURT (1922–2007)

An American writer primarily of novels and short stories, Vonnegut was born in Indianapolis, Indiana. He used his experiences as well as the beliefs and thinking of that Midwestern city in his writings. The effect of the Depression on his middle-class family produced a darkly comic voice, evident in his wildly successful novels *Slaughterhouse-Five* (1969) and *Cat's Cradle* (1963). Vonnegut was an activist on a number of issues, including nuclear-arms control and protection of the earth's biosphere. He said that he tried to be "a responsible elder in our society."

WALCOTT, DEREK (1930–2017)

Born on the island of Saint Lucia, a former British colony in the Caribbean, Walcott trained as an artist but also began writing poetry while still a boy. His work alternates between English and Caribbean patois and often serves as a bridge between the two cultures. He spent many years teaching and working in theatre in the United States but always kept his link to his home in Trinidad. He received a MacArthur Fellowship in 1981 and the Nobel Prize in Literature in 1992, and he published more than twenty books of poetry. His *Collected Poems 1948–1984* came out in 1986.

WALKER, ALICE (1944–)

Novelist and poet Alice Walker, the youngest of eight children, was born in Georgia to sharecropper parents. After attending segregated schools through high school, she received a scholarship to Spelman College and later matriculated at Sarah Lawrence College. Whatever her writing medium, her work deals in large part with race and gender issues. Among her many awards are a Pulitzer Prize for Fiction and a National Book Award for Fiction, both in 1983, for her novel *The Color Purple*. Her *Collected Poems* was published in 2005.

WHEELOCK, JOHN HALL (1886–1978)

Wheelock was born and grew up in New York City. After college he worked at publisher Charles Scribner's Sons, eventually succeeding renowned editor Maxwell Perkins as editor in chief. He initiated the Poets of Today series and was an advocate for the poets of his time. He is quoted as saying, "The function of the arts is to...make us suddenly reexperience something that we've always known but haven't been experiencing anymore." Among his fourteen published books of poetry is *This Blessed Earth: New and Selected Poems 1927–1977* (1978). His honors include the Bollingen Prize for Poetry.

WHITMAN, WALT (1819–1892)

Arguably America's most seminal poet, Whitman has affected almost every American bard since his time. He left school at eleven and worked as a printer for five years before turning to teaching and then journalism. Whitman's most important work, *Leaves of Grass* (1855), was self-published, and he continued working on it throughout his life. Ignored by most critics, the book was highly praised by Ralph Waldo Emerson, who wrote directly to Whitman. During the Civil War, Whitman served as a nurse for three years in the Washington, DC, area. His final work of poetry and prose, *Good-Bye My Fancy,* was published in 1891.

WILBUR, RICHARD (1921–2017)

Born in New York City, Wilbur was the grandson and great-grandson of editors and wrote for the college newspaper and magazine while attending Amherst College. After serving in the army during World War II, he began to write poetry as a means of coming to terms with his wartime experiences. As a formalist writer, using traditional rhyme and meter, Wilbur was never in the vanguard, but his well-crafted poems found a wide audience. He was the second Poet Laureate of the United States and won both the National Book Award and the Pulitzer Prize for Poetry in 1957 for *Things of This World* (1956).

WILLIAMS, C. K. (1936–2015)

A poet, translator, and critic, Williams grew up in New Jersey and started writing poetry while at the University of Pennsylvania. He was befriended by the architect Louis Kahn, who inspired him to embrace the artist's calling. After some false starts, Williams gradually began to use what he called "long, ragged lines" for his poems, which gave them their characteristic conversational tone and, in his words, "gave me a way to deal more inclusively and exhaustively with my own mind." He went on writing poetry until the end of his life, finishing his last book, *Falling Ill,* just twenty days before his death from multiple myeloma. Among his many honors were the Pulitzer Prize for Poetry in 2000 and the National Book Award for Poetry in 2003. *Selected Later Poems* was published in 2015.

WILLIAMS, WILLIAM CARLOS (1883–1963)

Williams was born in Rutherford, New Jersey, and lived there most of his life. After graduating from the University of Pennsylvania medical school, he became a family doctor and practiced for more than forty years. At the same time, he carried on a successful literary career, primarily as a poet but also writing fiction, plays, essays, and translations. He was known as a modernist, but in contrast to his contemporaries T. S. Eliot and Ezra Pound, he preferred to use colloquial American English and write about everyday experiences and objects. His famous phrase "No ideas but in things" summarized his poetic method. He won the first National Book Award for Poetry in 1950 for both the third volume of his epic poem *Paterson* and his *Selected Poems*. In 1963 he received the Pulitzer Prize posthumously for *Pictures from Brueghel and Other Poems* (1962).

YEATS, W. B. (1865–1939)

William Butler Yeats was one of the greatest poets of the twentieth century. As a dramatist and politician, he helped spur the Irish literary revival and served as a senator for the newborn Irish Free State. However, it is as a creator of beautiful and relevant poetry that his fame ultimately rests. Born into the Protestant, Anglo-Irish minority that had ruled Ireland for centuries, he nevertheless defined himself as staunchly Irish. While Yeats was fascinated with transcendental and occult themes in his early work, his later poems are more direct and accessible. He received the Nobel Prize in Literature in 1923. *The Collected Poems of W. B. Yeats* was published in 1996.

INDEX